ISSUE 6, JULY 2019

AUSTRALIAN FOREIGN AFFAIRS

Contributors

Elizabeth Becker is a former *New York Times* correspondent and the author of *When the War Was Over*.

Alison Broinowski is a former Australian diplomat and academic.

Sean Dorney is a Walkley Award–winning journalist and a nonresident fellow at the Lowy Institute.

Bill Farmer was Australian ambassador to Indonesia from 2005 to 2010.

Euan Graham is executive director of La Trobe Asia and former director of the international security program at the Lowy Institute.

Jenny Hayward-Jones is a nonresident fellow at the Lowy Institute.

Robert E. Kelly is a professor of international relations at Pusan National University in South Korea.

Kayleigh Long is a journalist who worked in Myanmar between 2013 and 2018 and is now based in London.

Katerina Teaiwa is an associate professor in the School of Culture, History and Language at the Australian National University.

Hugh White is a professor of strategic studies at the Australian National University and a former deputy secretary in the defence department.

Australian Foreign Affairs is published three times a year by Schwartz Publishing Pty Ltd. Publisher: Morry Schwartz. ISBN 978-1-76064-1542 ISSN 2208-5912 ALL RIGHTS RESERVED. No part of this publication may be reproduced, stored in a retrieval system, or transmitted in any form by any means, electronic, mechanical, photocopying, recording or otherwise, without the prior consent of the publishers. Essays, reviews and correspondence © retained by the authors. Subscriptions – 1 year print & digital auto-renew (3 issues): $49.99 within Australia incl. GST. 1 year print and digital subscription (3 issues): $59.99 within Australia incl. GST. 2 year print & digital (6 issues): $114.99 within Australia incl. GST. 1 year digital only auto-renew: $29.99. Payment may be made by MasterCard, Visa or Amex, or by cheque made out to Schwartz Publishing Pty Ltd. Payment includes postage and handling. To subscribe, fill out the form inside this issue, subscribe online at www.australianforeignaffairs.com, email subscribe@australianforeignaffairs.com or phone 1800 077 514 / 61 3 9486 0288. Correspondence should be addressed to: The Editor, Australian Foreign Affairs, Level 1, 221 Drummond Street, Carlton VIC 3053 Australia Phone: 61 3 9486 0288 / Fax: 61 3 9486 0244 Email: enquiries@australianforeignaffairs.com Editor: Jonathan Pearlman. Associate Editor: Chris Feik. Consulting Editor: Allan Gyngell. Deputy Editor: Julia Carlomagno. *AFA Weekly* editor: Dion Kagan. Management: Caitlin Yates. Marketing: Elisabeth Young, Georgia Mill and Iryna Byelyayeva. Publicity: Anna Lensky. Design: Peter Long. Production Coordination: Marilyn de Castro. Typesetting: Akiko Chan. Cover photo of aircraft by Olivier Ravenel/Armée de l'air/Armées. Printed in Australia by McPherson's Printing Group.

OUR SPHERE OF INFLUENCE

On 2 June 2019, Scott Morrison landed at Honiara International Airport in Solomon Islands for his first overseas visit since winning the federal election. This airport, on the northern coast of the island of Guadalcanal, was built in 1942 by Japanese troops as they tried to cut off supply lines between Australia and the United States, potentially allowing for an invasion of Australia. US troops eventually captured the airfield in a battle that marked the beginning of the Allied victory in the Pacific.

In April 2014, the airport was left underwater following the worst recorded flooding in the country's history. At least twenty-three people were killed and 50,000 were affected as the deluge – 73 centimetres of rain in three days – caused mudslides that destroyed villages, roads and livelihoods. The next year, Solomon Islands prime minister Manasseh Sogavare addressed the United Nations and declared that the threat of climate change to his country was "existential".

When Morrison arrived at Honiara, he was not there to discuss climate change. His concern, shaped by the legacy of World War II, was to prevent Solomon Islands again becoming a staging point for an attack on Australia. This is the unstated motivation for the "Pacific step-up", his signature foreign policy – to ensure that a foreign military presence is not installed in Australia's sphere of influence in the South Pacific. Today, this threat comes from China.

But this longstanding goal of Australian defence and foreign policy is now being challenged. Chinese aid and influence are spreading southward, just as Australia's diplomatic clout in the Pacific is coming under strain. Solomon Islands, whose largest trading partner is China, has recently signalled it may shift its diplomatic allegiance from Taiwan to China. And countries such as Papua New Guinea – a former Australian colony – are welcoming an increasing flow of Chinese funds. The prospect of a nearby Chinese military base is causing anxiety in Canberra, but Australia is still the largest Pacific donor, and presumes that recipients will see it as both a benefactor and a protector.

As part of his step-up, in 2018 Morrison visited Fiji and Vanuatu, the first diplomatic trip to either country by an Australian leader. This renewed Australian interest has been largely well received by Pacific states. The problem is that Australia and its neighbours currently view these two world-changing phenomena, China's rise and climate change, so differently. The success of the step-up will depend on whether Morrison can overcome this impasse. Even then, the future of Australia's sphere of influence will depend on whether – or for how long – China can be kept out of the region.

Jonathan Pearlman

IN DENIAL

Defending Australia
as China looks south

Hugh White

Let's be honest: Australians have never had much time for our South Pacific neighbours. The island nations that lie to our north and northeast, stretching from Papua New Guinea and Solomon Islands to Vanuatu, Fiji and beyond, may be close to us geographically, but we have not found them especially interesting, important or profitable. With a few honourable exceptions, and tourism aside, Australians have been indifferent to our nearest neighbours' dramatic landscapes, their rich and diverse cultures, and their general welfare, and we have seen relatively few opportunities for trade. Only their strategic significance has attracted us: the islands scattered widely across the north of our continent are critical to our protection from armed attack.

Our closest neighbours are crucial to the defence of our continent simply because of their proximity. Military operations are governed by distance, as distance defines what is operationally possible and what is affordable. Whether you can sink a ship, bomb an airfield or seize a town – and, critically, how much it will cost – depends on how far your forces must operate from their bases, and how far the enemy must operate from theirs. This has been true for as long as wars have been fought, and it remains true today. Cost and difficulty rise swiftly as the range at which forces must operate increases, because it means, for example, that aircraft must be refuelled mid-flight, or ships must operate beyond the range of land-based air cover, or larger and larger missiles must be fired at an exponentially increasing cost. Only cyber-attacks seem capable of breaking the nexus between geography and conflict, but it remains unclear whether they can match the strategic effect of actual violence. War remains a very physical business.

For much of our history, distance has worked to Australia's advantage. We have been secure because we are remote. None of the countries close to us has been strong enough to pose any serious threat, and the great powers that might have threatened us have been too far away to do so. But we lose this advantage if a potentially hostile great power can operate from bases close to our shores. This allows it to bring its strength to bear against us much more directly and effectively. We realise then that remoteness cuts both ways. It makes us feel vulnerable because we presume that the only credible reason for a major power to deploy forces to our remote corner of the world is to threaten us. It reminds us that we are far from our friends, too, and they may not be willing to come to our aid. And it means we must be prepared to meet such a threat by ourselves – something we have long assumed was beyond our capacity to do.

All this was clear to the British colonists who settled Australia in the eighteenth century. They brought with them an instinct for strategy distilled from centuries of experience. Britain's security had always depended on keeping the ports on the other side of the English Channel from the hands of powerful rivals who might use them to launch an invasion. They soon understood that Australia's security likewise depended on preventing any potentially hostile great power from acquiring bases in the arc of islands that stretches across Australia's north and out into the South Pacific. The western end of that archipelago was

Another rising and ambitious Asian power seems bent on intruding into our backyard

under Dutch control, which suited these British settlers fine: the Dutch were not strong enough to keep others out but not so strong as to threaten Australia. But until quite late in the nineteenth century, the islands east from New Guinea were, to English eyes, ungoverned territories that could be easily occupied by any great power who chose to do so.

This didn't matter much as long as Britain remained the unchallenged arbiter of strategic affairs globally, and especially in our corner of the Pacific. It mattered a lot more when the Pax Britannica started to fray in the 1870s and 1880s, and European powers such as France and Germany began to look for colonies in our backyard. Australian political leaders became concerned that such outposts in the South Pacific would provide these continental powers with bases from which to attack Australia. A new sense of Australia's distinct strategic interests and imperatives emerged as our leaders tried, and generally failed, to convince London to block these intrusions. It became clear that the colonies should do more to prepare for their own defence. Thus, the putative threat from French and German intrusions into the South Pacific played a large part in promoting the movement for Federation.

The threat from France or Germany never materialised, of course, and it disappeared completely when the cataclysm of World War I decimated these nations and their ability to project global power. But the strategic insight that underpinned these early anxieties was vindicated in 1942, when a rising, ambitious Asian nation brushed aside the remnants of British regional primacy, seized bases in the islands on Australia's doorstep and used them to threaten Australia directly for the first (and so far only) time in our history since European settlement. And now another rising and ambitious Asian power seems bent on intruding into our backyard, so all those anxieties are flaring again.

Adrift in the Pacific

"We would view with great concern the establishment of any foreign military bases in those Pacific Island countries and neighbours of ours." That was then prime minister Malcolm Turnbull in April 2018, responding to press reports that China might establish a naval base in

Vanuatu. But it could have been Henry Parkes writing to the British government in London in the 1870s, or Billy Hughes at the Versailles Peace Conference in 1919, or "Doc" Evatt at the United Nations' inaugural meeting in San Francisco in 1945. All saw this as Australia's primary strategic interest. And they all believed that the only way to deny a potential adversary access to bases in our immediate neighbourhood was to control these islands – or to persuade Britain to control them on Australia's behalf. From the period before Federation until the early 1960s, Australia's highest strategic priorities, and perhaps our most notable diplomatic triumphs, were focused on asserting and maintaining Australian or British colonial control of the islands closest to us, not because we much wanted them ourselves, but to deny them to anyone else.

But in the 1960s, as colonialism collapsed in every other corner of the globe, it became harder and harder to argue that Australia should rule our closest neighbours as colonial subjects indefinitely. Apart from the reputational costs, doing so would require a lot more money and effort than we had ever been willing to commit. The security imperative also seemed to be lessening. In the late 1960s and early 1970s, leading figures in Australian strategic debate such as Tom Millar, Hedley Bull, Peter Hastings and Owen Harries argued that the islands to our north were becoming less important to our security. Fear of a return to militarism in Japan, which remained potent for years after 1945, had largely dissipated, and China no longer seemed a threat. It had never possessed significant maritime power, and after the rapprochement with the United States in 1972 it ceased to pose a challenge to Australia's allies or strategic interests. Asia entered a long period of unprecedented peace and prosperity in which both the wider regional order and Australia's security were supported by uncontested American primacy. For the first time since British power in Asia had begun to wane, Australia had no real reason to fear that a potential adversary might seek to threaten us from island bases in the north. And so it was that Australia quite willingly saw our little empire in Papua New Guinea, and Britain's colonies in Solomon Islands, Vanuatu (shared with France), Fiji and the rest, pass into history and our close neighbours emerge as independent sovereign states.

The plan, insofar as there was one, was for Australia to protect its residual interests in the South Pacific by establishing itself as the natural leader of these new states, becoming their principal diplomatic partner, and their guide and protector in world affairs. In short, we would build a "sphere of influence" to take the place of our colonial empire, and thereby exclude any threatening intrusions. It seemed a credible idea. After all, we had a lot going for us. We were the region's largest aid donor and major economic partner. Our neighbours' apparent commitment to democracy and Western values seemed to ensure a natural alignment of interests, and our former colonial role had left, we believed, deep reservoirs of goodwill and gratitude towards us. And we – along with New Zealand – were the only countries prepared to show an interest in them, while for them our alliance with the United States seemed to offer a connection with the dominant superpower.

The assumption was that these countries, with our help, would swiftly evolve into functioning independent states well-disposed to Australia and willing to accept it as the regional leader. But that is not how things turned out. Development has been slow, governments have faced repeated meltdowns and Australia's attention has been episodic, at best. Among our foreign and strategic policy communities, and in formal policy statements such as White Papers, there has always been a clear acknowledgement that we have a vital strategic interest in these countries. For example, the Howard government's 2000 Defence White Paper stated bluntly, "We have a key interest in helping to prevent the positioning in neighbouring states of foreign forces that might be used

Our relations with our Pacific island neighbours have become increasingly estranged

to attack Australia." But in the benign Asia of recent decades, there has been virtually no chance that this interest would be challenged, and thus little pressure. Crises such as the Fiji coups or Papua New Guinea's Sandline affair have commanded Canberra's attention for a few weeks or months. The high point in Australian engagement was our leadership of the Regional Assistance Mission to Solomon Islands (RAMSI): a fourteen-year, multi-billion-dollar program to stabilise Solomon Islands and reconstruct key institutions of state. But between crises, Australia's engagement has been uninspiring, with the key point of contact largely the aid program.

And so over nearly fifty years our relations with our Pacific island neighbours have become increasingly estranged, due to lack of interest in Canberra and consequent disenchantment among our neighbours. Australia's sphere of influence in the South Pacific has become threadbare, depending for its credibility on the fact that no one has tried to challenge it.

The China wake-up call

Last April's press report that China was seeking to build a naval base in Vanuatu was not the first sign that things were changing in the South Pacific. For a decade now, China has been emerging as a major aid donor and investor in the region, and policymakers and analysts in Canberra have been uneasily aware that its influence is increasing. But the challenge this presents to Australia's position in the South Pacific has been somewhat obscured by Canberra's reluctance to, until very recently, acknowledge that China poses a genuine threat to the US-led regional order.

For a long time, the oft-repeated mantra "we don't have to choose between America and China" reflected a complacent assumption that China would not seriously aim to displace America and to establish its own sphere of influence in East Asia and the Western Pacific. That, in turn, encouraged complacency about the prospect that China was intent on challenging our sphere of influence in the South Pacific. Only in 2017 did Australian political leaders start to acknowledge the scale of China's regional ambitions. Julie Bishop's speech to the

Fullerton Forum in Singapore in April that year, and Malcolm Turnbull's address to the Shangri-La Dialogue, also in Singapore, that June, rang the official first alarm bells about China's objectives. Turnbull alluded to the idea that China was seeking to establish a Monroe Doctrine–style regional hegemony at America's – and Australia's – expense. Canberra was therefore already getting worried before reports came in about China's plans for a military base near us.

The story was broken by Fairfax's foreign affairs correspondent David Wroe, under the headline "China eyes Vanuatu military base in plan with global ramifications". He wrote of "preliminary discussions between the Chinese and Vanuatu governments about a military build-up in the island nation". It is unlikely that Wroe's article came as a surprise to the Australian government. Indeed, the government was probably its major source: Wroe cited "senior security officials" as believing that while no "formal proposals" had yet been made by the Chinese, "Beijing's plans could culminate in a full military base".

The story was swiftly and categorically denied by both Beijing and Port Vila, and Julie Bishop, then Minister for Foreign Affairs, poured cold water on it. Nonetheless, Turnbull took the report seriously enough to issue a stern warning, and it apparently captured Scott Morrison's attention, prompting some major new policy initiatives from Canberra. While the Vanuatu story may prove a false alarm, it seems Canberra has received credible indications that China is indeed actively seeking a military base somewhere in the South

Pacific. It would be hard to overstate the significance of such a development, were it to occur. This would be the first time since Japan was pushed out of the islands at the end of the Pacific War that any major power, other than one of our allies, has sought a military base so close to Australia. It must shape the judgements we make, both about China's military capacity and intentions towards Australia, and about the probability and scale of a direct military attack on our shores in the years ahead. If China really is considering a South Pacific base, what does it say about the nation's ambitions and intentions, and how should Australia respond?

China looks south

Why would China want a military base in the South Pacific? Foreign military bases have not traditionally been a feature of its strategic posture. The only overseas military base Beijing acknowledges is a facility in Djibouti, on the coast of Africa. That was set up in 2015, primarily, it seems, to support Chinese participation in international anti-piracy operations off the Horn of Africa.

There has been talk of Chinese plans to establish naval facilities elsewhere in the Indian Ocean – in Myanmar, Sri Lanka and Pakistan especially – under the guise of civilian port projects. Often referred to as the 'string of pearls', these ports have supposedly been built to allow China to project maritime power into the Indian Ocean, to challenge both India's regional ambitions and the United States' long-standing maritime preponderance there. Port facilities built and operated by

China plainly could be used to support military operations – if host governments agreed. But there is little evidence that this is China's plan, and it would not make much military sense, because in any significant conflict with India or the United States, such bases would have little value.

China's increasingly formidable maritime forces are not primarily designed to project power far from its shores. Their main purpose is to resist power projection into China's near approaches, by targeting an adversary's ships and aircraft and the local bases from which they would operate. This is clever, because it puts China on the right side of the contest between offence and defence in maritime warfare. Today, pro-

This is no longer America's lake, and is fast becoming China's instead

jecting power requires large and costly vessels such as aircraft carriers, and these are vulnerable to missile and torpedo attack – which is much cheaper to mount than in the past. That makes it relatively easy for China to stop the United States from advancing into China's Western Pacific approaches, but hard for China to project power into distant theatres. In the Indian Ocean, for example, China's ships and planes would be vulnerable to US or Indian naval and air forces, and in a serious clash any bases there could be swiftly and easily destroyed. The same would be true in the South Pacific. In a war against a well-armed adversary, an isolated military base in our region could quickly be put out of action, its supply lines to China interdicted, and the air and naval forces based there left vulnerable to attack. It would soon be more a liability than an asset.

But this narrow operational perspective is not the only way to look at the role of military bases. We can see why China may want a base in the South Pacific when we look at its broader military posture and how this relates to its strategic ambitions. A facility with little military value can carry diplomatic weight as a symbol of intention and resolve, and that can be important strategically. China does not want to fight a major war to achieve its goal of primacy in the Western Pacific, because it hopes and expects to be able to convince others to accept its power more or less peacefully. But to do that, China has to convince the region of its capacity, and the resolve to impose its will if necessary. That is what it has been doing in the South China Sea. China's bases on contested features such as Mischief Reef would be of little use in a serious conflict, because they would be easy to knock out in the first few hours of a clash. Their value to China is in showing the world, including the United States and its allies and friends in Asia, how serious China is about defying US power and asserting itself as a maritime player in the Western Pacific – showing that this is no longer America's lake, and is fast becoming China's instead.

If China is looking to build a military base in Vanuatu, Papua New Guinea or Solomon Islands, this seems the most plausible explanation of its motives. In fact, such a move would make sense from Beijing's perspective. It is unlikely that China seriously expects to dominate the Indian Ocean, given India's strong position there; it is much more likely that the nation aims to bring the whole Western Pacific region, including Australia's northern island neighbours, within its sphere of influence. That's because great powers tend to expand their spheres to the geographical point where they meet resistance from another great power. If Beijing can convince the United States to step back from the Western Pacific, it can reasonably anticipate extending its sway over Melanesia, Micronesia and Polynesia without confronting another great power. Establishing a base in our neighbourhood would be a low-cost, low-risk way to show off its growing military and diplomatic reach and clout. Moreover, by ignoring the noisy complaints that would surely emanate from Washington, Beijing would show that it is willing to defy the United States. And it would send an unambiguous message to us here in Australia, signalling Beijing's rejection of our claims to our own sphere of influence in the South Pacific, and sending a stark warning of China's reach and its capacity to punish us if we side too vociferously with the United States or Japan against it.

Looking further ahead, it would provide a useful foundation for the kind of regional posture that China might be planning to adopt once it has established itself as the Western Pacific's dominant power. Then China would be able to not merely block advancing rivals but also project power by sea, just as the United States has been able to do for so long because until recently no other nation was game or powerful enough to try to stop it. This helps explain why China is investing in aircraft carriers even though it knows how vulnerable they would be in any war against a major rival. It is preparing for the day when it has no major rivals in the Western Pacific. And come that day, a base in our backyard could be quite handy for the kind of lower-level 'policing' operations that a preponderant power must be prepared to do from time to time among the nations over which it exercises hegemony.

China next door

How hard would it be for China to find a military base in the South Pacific? We can perhaps exclude, for the time being, the question of whether it could acquire one by force, and focus instead on its chances of securing permission from one of our near neighbours to establish a site on their sovereign territory.

We would be unwise to assume this would be difficult.

Of course, there are many good reasons for our neighbours to resist such a request. There are principles of high policy: the Vanuatu government, in denying the Fairfax story, said that its commitment to non-alignment precluded the hosting of foreign bases on its soil. More importantly, our neighbours have developed alignments with Western, and specifically Australian, perspectives and interests, which have carried over from the colonial era and have been perpetuated under the United States' clear and mostly benevolent supremacy. Perhaps more important still are fears of getting too close to a country as powerful and potentially as demanding as China.

Relatively small and vulnerable nations, our neighbours would likely be concerned about interference in their internal affairs, and of being drawn into China's rivalries with other powers. Finally, they would worry about what Australia, the United States and perhaps other allies, such as Japan, might do to punish them for siding with China – and how their South Pacific neighbours might react, too.

But these factors would likely be outweighed by what China can offer – and what it can threaten. China's growing wealth and power give it huge influence. In the years to come it will increasingly overtake Australia and other Western-oriented countries as the most important economic partner for our small neighbours. It will become the primary source of

The new Manus base is just a bit of flag-showing

trade, investment and aid, and Beijing will decide which opportunities are offered and which withheld. The benefits of acquiescing to a Chinese base might simply be too great to refuse. Moreover, any assenting states may assume that they can rely on Australia and the United States to counterbalance Chinese influence, or that they can play us and the Chinese off against each other. Nor are national interests the only consideration here. Beijing will no doubt be willing to offer personal inducements to leaders willing to see things their way.

Our neighbours' commitment to values and interests shared with Australia might prove feeble in the face of Chinese persuasion. We'd be unwise to expect that their gratitude for our generous aid in decades past will outweigh their anticipation of future benefits flowing from Beijing. Their recollections of all we have done for them will be counterbalanced by equally vivid recollections of Australia's record of interference, paternalism and neglect. They will note that Australia is eager to take advantage of its own economic opportunities in China, and has been willing to trim its policy sails to do so – which might make our protests about their accommodations with Beijing look distinctly hypocritical. And they will ask why they should be sensitive to our strategic concerns about China when we have been so insensitive to their fears about climate change – an issue on which China's credentials might seem somewhat better than ours.

Denial in the South Pacific

What can Australia do, then, to restore and preserve our sphere of influence in the South Pacific, and deny it to China? Our government has at least taken the first step by recognising that there is a problem. It is now clearly understood that Australia can no longer take our influence for granted. Instead we face a classic contest for influence against the region's, and perhaps soon the world's, most powerful country. That contest is part of something even bigger – a challenge as to who will preside over the wider East Asian and Western Pacific region. We have been here before, of course. Despite our remoteness, Australia is again, as we were in 1942, on the front line of a major contest over the future of Asia. Scott Morrison seems to understand this, and he has made the South Pacific his signature foreign policy priority.

But practical policy steps? The centrepiece of the Morrison government's strategy so far is the announcement, at last year's APEC Summit in Port Moresby, of plans to develop a naval base on Manus Island, in partnership with the United States. Manus played a significant role as a US base in the Pacific War, but it is not clear what exactly a new base there will do for us. Perhaps Morrison hopes that US involvement, announced at APEC by Vice President Mike Pence, will deter China from seeking to build a strategic presence in our backyard. If so, he misunderstands the nature of the United States–China rivalry in Asia. Beijing *seeks* opportunities to compete with America for position and influence in the Western Pacific, as we have seen in the East and South China Seas, because such contests provide China with opportunities to display its growing power and reach, and to demonstrate its willingness to confront Washington. US involvement in the Manus base and in other initiatives to counter growing Chinese influence may well encourage rather than deter Beijing in its efforts. So, diplomatically the initiative could prove counter-productive, even if the United States is seriously committed to it – which, in Trump's Washington, is not to be taken for granted.

In operational terms, a base on Manus would be of little use to defend Papua New Guinea from China. Canberra and Washington seem only to be contemplating a simple facility that could support light forces such as patrol boats, small warships and maritime surveillance aircraft for low-level peacetime operations. Building facilities to support high-level air and naval operations would cost many billions of dollars, and no one is talking about that kind of money. If they were, it is far from clear that Manus would be the best place to spend it. A campaign to defend Papua New Guinea from Chinese attack would primarily involve submarine and air operations, for which Manus is in many ways poorly suited. So the new Manus base is, in reality, just a bit of flag-showing. It raises a fundamental question: under what circumstances would we be willing to fight to keep China out of our immediate neighbourhood? That needs a lot of thought, but it is clear that we would not, as things stand, fight to prevent China setting up a military base if it was doing so with the agreement of a host government. So it is doubtful that a facility on Manus will do anything to prevent China seeking and securing a base of its own in Papua New Guinea or elsewhere in our region, or to limit its influence there more broadly.

Canberra's second big initiative has been to try to counterbalance China's growing aid program – especially large-scale infrastructure projects under the sprawling Belt and Road Initiative – by setting up, with Washington and Tokyo, a rival fund for infrastructure projects in the South Pacific. This is an obvious move, but not necessarily a smart one, because it will be hard to beat China in this game. Its pockets are deeper and its expertise in building infrastructure is now formidable. And while we accuse China of building expensive glamour projects that buy political influence while doing little for economic and social development, we may well find ourselves doing the same thing. Long experience – for example, with Papua New Guinea's Highlands Highway – tells us that infrastructure projects alone achieve little. Development is much harder than simply building a bridge.

The third initiative in Australia's pushback against Chinese encroachment is using the South Pacific's multilateral forums to mobilise opposition to Beijing's growing influence and to bolster support for Canberra's regional leadership. This has so far met a very mixed response. Some Pacific island countries are worried by China's growing power, but reluctant to become pawns in a contest of great-power politics. This is symbolised by the islands' rejection of the label "Indo-Pacific".

We should start to treat our smaller close neighbours as independent at last

This concept, so dear to policymakers in Canberra, Washington and Tokyo, frames the region as united in resisting China's hegemonic ambitions. Pacific islanders have preferred to sidestep this by talking instead of the "Blue Pacific", an evocative but vague concept that shifts the focus from geostrategic rivalries and towards the unique challenges, particularly rising sea levels, that nations with small territories but vast oceanic areas face. The reality is that our South Pacific neighbours do not see the contest with China the same way we do.

Abandoning the sphere of influence

Nothing we are doing so far seems to be working. What might we do instead?

One option is a radical recasting of our relations and role in the South Pacific, to draw our neighbours much more closely under our wing. Ever since their intractable post-independence problems became obvious in the late 1980s, it has been natural to wonder whether it might be possible to turn the clock back, if only halfway. No one contemplates re-colonisation, of course, but might there be some new model of engagement that gives Canberra a far larger and more effective role in these nations' development, towards which RAMSI might point the way? This could address barriers to development that our neighbours have been unable to overcome as independent states, and vastly strengthen our capacity to keep potential enemies out of range of our territory.

Yet, leaving aside the question of how and why our neighbours might be induced to consent to such an arrangement, the cost to Australia would be enormous. It might be the only way to preserve the kind of sphere of influence that generations of Australian policymakers have believed to be essential for our security, but that doesn't make it a credible policy option. It may instead simply confirm that our assumptions about our regional influence are no longer realistic.

The better option would be to step back, abandoning our traditional ideas about keeping intruders out of the South Pacific. In fact, there may be no alternative. China poses an unprecedented challenge to the strategic assumptions that have framed our policies since European settlement. We have never encountered an Asian country as powerful as China is now, let alone as powerful as it will likely become in the decades ahead. Its ambitions constitute a far bigger threat to US leadership in Asia than ever before, and a far bigger threat to Australia's position in the South Pacific than we have ever faced. The costs to us of trying to keep China out of the region might simply prove impossible to bear. Or, to be more precise, it might prove cheaper to build military capabilities that in a war could neutralise Chinese bases in the South Pacific (by denying access to them and subjecting them to strike attacks) than to prevent China from establishing such bases in peacetime.

We probably need to build those forces anyway, because the capabilities we would need are much the same as those required to independently defend our territory from a major power – a possibility we need to consider as America's position in Asia fades. The sobering reality is that China will likely succeed in pushing the United States out and taking its place as the primary power in the Western Pacific – and not just because of Trump. The costs and risks to America of maintaining its position in the region may soon exceed its interests. To defend ourselves without US support, we need to focus on developing the capability to protect our air and sea approaches from hostile forces, and to attack bases and lodgements on our territory or close to our shores. If we are serious about our security, we should start building these forces now.

Building forces that could counter Chinese bases in our neighbourhood would mean that we could feel less anxious about the establishment of such bases, and relax the imperative to preserve the sphere of influence we have for so long assumed we must maintain. This would not mean abandoning all interest in our nearest neighbours and succumbing to the indifference that has historically weakened our relationships with them. On the contrary, we should make great efforts to maximise our role and presence – not in the form of an exclusive sphere of influence, but as one of the region's major partners. It is possible to imagine Australia actively engaged in the South Pacific not to exclude China (or any other power), but to work with it where possible, and to work against it where necessary, to protect our interests and the interests we share with our small neighbours as best we can. We should start to treat our smaller close neighbours as independent at last. We shouldn't expect to exercise any crude veto over their foreign policies and relations, but we should seek to influence their decisions in the way we seek to influence our larger neighbours in South-East Asia. Soberingly, that will require more effort on our part, not less, despite the more modest objectives, because our engagement in the South Pacific has been so weak for so long.

The uncomfortable reality is that preserving an exclusive sphere of influence in the South Pacific is not going to be possible against a regional power that is far stronger than any we have ever confronted, or even contemplated. It might turn out that the more we try and fail to exclude China from the South Pacific, the less influence we will have there. Recognising and accepting the inescapable reality of China's power will enable us to respond more effectively. A more complex and demanding kind of engagement than any we have known since we relinquished colonial rule is what is needed in the new Asia of the twenty-first century.

We are only just realising that the rise of China changes everything in Australia's international environment, and that our foreign policy has to adapt accordingly. So far our governments have tried to respond with as little change as possible. Scott Morrison will find, as he settles into his first term as an elected prime minister, that embracing rather than evading change will be the biggest challenge he faces. If he is as serious about the South Pacific as he claims, he should start, perhaps paradoxically, by abandoning the idea of an exclusive sphere of influence, and then guide Australians to take a much greater interest in our neighbourhood than we ever have before. ■

CROSS PURPOSES

Why is Australia's Pacific influence waning?

Jenny Hayward-Jones

The practice of Australian foreign policy in the Pacific islands region is based on an assumption that the national interests of Australia and Pacific island countries are broadly similar. Pacific islands share with Australia custodianship of the same ocean, membership of the Pacific Islands Forum, Westminster parliamentary traditions and a history of cooperation to advance the region's interests.

Australia's dominance as an aid donor, investor and trading partner in the region has helped its policies and initiatives win acceptance from Pacific island governments. Peace, stability and prosperity in the Pacific islands region is supposed to be everyone's goal, and on this basis, Australian diplomats have urged Pacific island governments to support Australian policies designed to achieve these mutually desired outcomes. Pacific island officials have in the past been reluctant to give voice to interests that conflict with Australia's in conversation with their counterparts. But over the last five years, as perceptions of Australia's influence have changed, as China's visibility has grown, as the climate change threat has worsened and as Pacific island leaders have become more assertive on the public stage, Australia has found its assumptions about the region challenged. For the nation, this marks a new – and more difficult – era of Pacific diplomacy.

Australia's Pacific diplomacy

The way that Canberra manages its relationships with Pacific island states has long been different from the way it manages relations with other countries. Australia has tended to view its Pacific island neighbours as predominantly poor, weak and fragile states, aid clients with limited agency. Australia has been the key donor in the region by a significant margin for most of the period in which these island states have been independent. Such dominance by one donor in one region is rare globally, similar only to the position the United States has enjoyed in the Middle East.

Australian diplomats based in Pacific islands carry out their work in very different circumstances to their colleagues in Asia, Europe or North America. Australian banks are prominent on the main streets of the capitals, and Australian judges sit regularly, along with some from other countries, on the benches of national courts of appeal. Three countries in the region (Kiribati, Nauru and

Tuvalu) use the Australian dollar as their currency. In Papua New Guinea, television audiences can watch Australian stations, and Australian rugby league teams have huge local fan bases. Australian diplomats serving in cities such as Port Moresby, Honiara and Port Vila are featured regularly in local newspapers and radio broadcasts opening aid projects or giving speeches promoting the importance of Australian aid in the community. They have the kind of profile in their host countries that members of parliament enjoy in Australia – a situation certainly not replicated for their counterparts posted elsewhere in the world.

China has given island states choices, reducing Australia's leverage

This dynamic creates an immediate inequality. Australian diplomats do not, as a matter of course, use the promise of aid as an inducement to secure commitments from their Pacific island counterparts, and Pacific island officials do not typically make decisions due to fears they may lose out on aid. But it is not possible to say that this never happens. Both parties in the relationship conduct conversations based on the assumption that the Australian holds leverage that the Pacific islander does not.

As a Department of Foreign Affairs and Trade (DFAT) third secretary in Port Vila many years ago, it was part of my job to lobby Vanuatu Ministry of Foreign Affairs officials to support Australian positions at the United Nations, and to negotiate with local officials to secure access for Australian goods and services as part of Vanuatu's process of joining the World Trade Organization. These types of tasks are performed by diplomats across the world. But in Vanuatu, as in other Pacific island countries, they are often overshadowed by Australia's dominance.

I once called on the Vanuatu Ministry of Foreign Affairs to lobby for Vanuatu's support for a resolution that Australia was sponsoring at the United Nations. It was not on a controversial issue, and the foreign ministry readily agreed to support Australia's position. But then my counterpart told me that the telephones at the ministry had been disconnected due to non-payment of bills, and they had no way of instructing Vanuatu's UN representative to attend the relevant session and cast a vote. I asked if I could help pass on the instructions via Australian channels, and my counterpart prepared a note for me to fax from the Australian High Commission to Vanuatu's office in New York. I did so, but I couldn't help wondering how I would feel in his position – if I was in Canberra and had to ask, for example, a US diplomat to send instructions to my colleagues in another country because I lacked the means to do so.

Pacific island governments have historically relied on Australia to fill in gaps in government services, provide emergency funding and respond to crises, and Australian diplomats were accustomed to being called on by their host governments to solve problems. There was an unwritten understanding that Pacific island governments who regularly called on Australia for help were also (generally) supportive of Australian foreign and trade policy initiatives. But this situation is changing. The increasing influence of other powers in Pacific island capitals will alter the way Australian diplomats do business. Australia can no longer expect that shared values and interests will induce Pacific island governments to support its policies. The effective climate advocacy by Pacific island governments has proven they do not need Australia's backing to promote their national interests on the world stage. China's growing aid, trade and investment has given island states choices, reducing Australia's leverage. Australian ministers and diplomats will need to work harder to convince their Pacific island counterparts to back its policy choices.

Australia first, then the neighbours

Although Australia has a proud history of leading the Pacific islands region, it has been slow to recognise the changing interests and needs of these states and their populations.

At annual Pacific Islands Forum leaders' summits, Australia, often in tandem with New Zealand, has traditionally made sure that the language in the communiqué and the major outcomes reflects Australia's priorities, even at the expense of the wishes of Pacific island states. For example, Australia has succeeded every year in watering down the language around climate change in the communiqué – though it was unable to do so at the last leaders' summit, held in Nauru in September 2018.

Pacific island states have lobbied Australia since the 1990s to allow their citizens to work in Australia on a seasonal basis in the horticultural sector, only to be continually rebuffed. In 2007, New Zealand initiated a program that allowed up to 5000 seasonal labourers to work for periods of up to seven months in its horticulture and viticulture sectors. Australia reluctantly decided in 2009 to introduce the Pacific Seasonal Worker Pilot Scheme to its horticulture sector, but has been slow to appreciate that such initiatives serve its interests as much as those of Pacific island countries. It was only last year that Australia introduced the more generous Pacific Labour Scheme, which allows Pacific islanders to work in rural and regional Australia for up to three years.

From 2009, Australia and New Zealand spent eight years negotiating a free trade agreement known as PACER Plus with nine Pacific island states. The deal, signed in 2017, did not provide much satisfaction to any of the parties. Island-state signatories were frustrated that Australia and New Zealand would not enshrine provisions for labour mobility. The two largest trading nations, Papua New Guinea and Fiji, refused to sign because they saw little economic benefit.

Australia's decision to establish and maintain detention centres on Nauru and Manus was driven entirely by the political interests of the Australian government. These centres were put into operation with little consideration of local laws or the impact on local people. The harmful effects not only on detained asylum seekers but also on society and governance in Nauru and Papua New Guinea, and the consequent challenges in Australia's management of its relations with both countries, are now obvious.

In its aid program, Australia has largely maintained a focus on governance and strengthening state institutions despite evidence to show this approach isn't working and island governments are desperate for better infrastructure. Canberra is troubled about law and order and poor policing, while Pacific islanders are more concerned about their failing health and education services.

Even in relatively straightforward diplomatic business, Canberra is driven to address Australia's concerns, not those of its neighbours. Several years ago, a senior Australian official in Port Moresby complained to me that

Pacific island leaders are now more willing to question Canberra's analysis

it was proving difficult to identify local officials with sufficient knowledge and experience to participate in a planned high-level dialogue with Australian defence and security experts. Having been involved in several such dialogues initiated by Australia, I suspected this problem had arisen because the Canberra-drafted agenda was focused on Australia's preoccupations about international security, rather than on Papua New Guinea's security concerns. Forums such as these should be designed to build trust and cooperation over time, not to make it harder for the other side to engage.

The threats from within

Long before Canberra's concerns about the potential threat to the region from China, the Australian government frequently described developments or circumstances in one or another Pacific island country as a security threat – to Australia or to the region.

Prime Minister John Howard said in 2003 that the Australian-led Regional Assistance Mission to Solomon Islands was partly aimed at reducing the risk that vulnerable Pacific island states could become havens for transnational crime, including terrorism. Australia and New Zealand led protests against the 2006 military coup in Fiji and the authoritarian rule of military commander Josaia Voreqe (Frank) Bainimarama because the breakdown of democracy was seen as a threat to the stability of the region. The 2017 Foreign Policy White Paper asserted that "stability in Papua New Guinea, the wider Pacific and Timor-Leste" was vital to Australia's "ability to defend our northern approaches, secure our borders and protect our exclusive economic zone".

In an interview with *ABC News* in April 2019, Nick Warner, Australia's Director-General of National Intelligence, mentioned Papua New Guinea among the security risks to Australia, which included North Korea and competition between China and the United States: "A country now of eight or nine million people, in twenty years plus it's going to be a population of 20 million. And its issues and problems will impact more directly on Australia than at any time since independence in 1975." Australian officials worry that poor law and order in

Papua New Guinea may eventually require intervention from Australia, that weak border security will encourage people-smuggling across the Torres Strait, that diseases such as tuberculosis and polio will spread, that Chinese investment in Papua New Guinea will damage Australia's economic interests, and that Papua New Guineans will seek a better life in Australia.

The Papua New Guinean government will almost certainly struggle to manage the demands of its growing population. In theory, this puts its national stability at risk, which in turn increases the perceived risk to Australia's national security. In practice, however, there is little evidence in the modern era that instability in one island country has provoked instability elsewhere in the region, or that Australia's national security has been undermined by conflict or other security failings in the Pacific.

Pacific island governments have always listened to Australia's anxieties about regional threats. But changing dynamics in the region, the confidence of island states to define their own strategic priorities and Australia's reputation for worrying about threats that have not ultimately affected Pacific island communities has meant that Pacific island leaders are now more willing to question Canberra's analysis. They may not so readily back Australia's new anxieties about China's growing influence.

The climate rift

Australia's interpretation of national security is somewhat different to that of its Pacific neighbours. Recently, the Australian government was so alarmed about the threat to its internet security posed by Huawei, the Chinese telecommunications giant that had negotiated contracts to build undersea cables from Solomon Islands and Papua New Guinea to the Australian mainland, that it intervened with both governments to take over the contracts. But for many Pacific island nations, there is a greater anxiety than shifting power dynamics in the region.

Pacific island leaders have repeatedly told their Australian counterparts that climate change is an existential threat to their populations. Back in 2014, for instance, Tuvalu prime minister Enele Sopoaga said climate change was "like a weapon of mass destruction" and warned Australia not to hamper international negotiations for what eventually became the Paris Agreement. In May 2017, Marshall Islands president Hilda Heine questioned Australia's standing in the Pacific due to its inaction on climate change. In October 2018, the secretary general of the Pacific Islands Forum, Dame Meg Taylor, discussed Australia's energy policy in a speech in Canberra, emphasising that "we cannot afford to have one or two of us acting in ways that place the wellbeing and potential of the Blue Pacific Continent at risk". And in January 2019, during Prime Minister Scott Morrison's visit to Fiji, Prime Minister Frank Bainimarama urged Australia to shift away from fossil fuels to guarantee the survival of Pacific island countries. In a Facebook message congratulating Morrison on his election win in May 2019, Bainimarama invited the prime minister to work closely with him in the global fight against climate change – "the most urgent crisis facing not only the Pacific but the world".

In contrast, Australian leaders tell their Pacific island counterparts they need Australian help in managing domestic and foreign security risks. Climate change comes second. The 2016 Defence White Paper names the challenges Pacific island countries will face over the next two to three decades as "population growth, ethnic tensions, political stability, governance capacity, environmental degradation and natural disasters". It also warns that "countries from outside the

Australia needs to do more than increase defence and aid spending

South Pacific will seek to expand their influence in the region, including through enhanced security ties". The 2017 Foreign Policy White Paper states that most countries in the Pacific islands face acute development and governance challenges, making it difficult for them to respond to a range of issues, including "transnational crime, natural disasters, climate change or outbreaks of infectious diseases". "This in turn exposes Australia to increased threats, which our cooperation helps to mitigate," the paper says.

Australia has often referred to climate change as a lower-order challenge for Pacific island countries, rather than the complex and pervasive crisis it is for the region. In the 2017 Foreign Policy White Paper, Australia's commitment to strengthen the "capacity of the Pacific, particularly low-lying atoll states, to respond to climate change" and promise of "$300 million over four years to provide climate science and data and other support to help our partners plan for and adapt to climate change and mitigate its impacts" is not among the top priorities of Australia's "new approach"; nor is climate change acknowledged as a security issue. Prime Minister Scott Morrison's decision to cease payments to the UN's Green Climate Fund was an unambiguous indication of the low priority he attached to the climate emergency in the region. The fund was working well for Pacific island states and was one of the few mechanisms Australia had to leverage more international financing to support resilience in the region.

Although recent DFAT statements have indicated that Australia is working to integrate climate change and disaster considerations into its aid investments across the Pacific, recognition of the centrality of the climate risk has been largely missing from Australian policy statements. The Australian government is afraid Pacific islanders don't appreciate the nature of the security threat the region faces. Pacific islanders are afraid the security threat the region faces will end life as they know it.

The 2019 Lowy Institute Poll found that Australians have, for the first time, ranked climate change at the top of a list of twelve possible threats to Australia's vital interests in the next ten years. Scott Morrison's government may point to its recent electoral success to justify domestic inaction on energy and climate policy, but Australia cannot continue to make foreign and security policy at cross-purposes with the interests of its Pacific neighbours or, indeed, of its own population.

Stepping up but staying put

To strengthen Pacific partnerships, Australia needs to do more than increase defence and aid spending in the region. In the DFAT document outlining Australia's "step-up" in the Pacific, "climate change and responding to natural disasters" is listed as one of four significant long-term challenges, but there is scant detail about measures to assist Australia's neighbours to deal with this challenge.

Australia is the principal aid donor and security partner in the region of the world most vulnerable to climate change, but has not exercised leadership on climate change in its diplomatic, aid or security planning. In contrast, a recent report by the UK parliament's International Development Committee recommended that the United Kingdom "must place climate change at the centre of aid strategy and funding". The report states that "climate change is not just one of a number of issues that the UK should address through aid spending, it is the single biggest threat to stability and wellbeing in some of the world's most vulnerable nations", and warns that the "failure to act will be so serious as to nullify the effectiveness of wider aid spending". The committee also called for a "joined-up approach" across government, recommending that UK Export Finance (the government export credits agency) cease providing support for fossil-fuel projects in developing countries.

Australia now spends more on aid in the Pacific islands than in any other region. Canberra will provide a record $1.4 billion to Pacific island countries in the 2019–20 financial year, through programs to support governance, infrastructure and trade, education, health, building resilience, agriculture, fisheries and water. Defence's contribution to the step-up in the region includes the gifting of and ongoing support for – to the value of $2 billion – nineteen Guardian-class patrol boats, military cooperation programs, the Australia Pacific Security College in Fiji, and the Lombrum Joint Initiative, which proposes to redevelop the naval base on Manus. Australian taxpayers are entitled to question why such a significant financial commitment does not have at its heart the goal of addressing the principal threat to the region's stability and wellbeing.

Australia and New Zealand have a history of operating in lock step in managing relations within the Pacific. Officials in Canberra and Wellington consult regularly, and their diplomats work together closely in Pacific island capitals. The two nations cooperated in the Bougainville peacekeeping operation and in the Regional Assistance Mission to Solomon Islands.

Both governments last year announced new approaches to the Pacific. The Australian policy is named "Stepping up our engagement in the Pacific", and New Zealand's is known as the "Pacific Reset".

The policies are motivated by concern about the growth of

China's influence and by the need to do more to demonstrate to Pacific island countries that they can offer the kind of support nations outside the region cannot. There are, however, some key differences between Australia's and New Zealand's handling of Pacific diplomacy. New Zealand has strong cultural affinities with island countries. Its significant Maori and Pacific populations allow it to project a Pacifica identity that Australia could never claim. As foreign minister Winston Peters has said, close ties to the Cook Islands and Niue, special connections with Samoa and Tonga, and responsibilities for the atoll islands of Tokelau permit New Zealand to claim membership of the "Pacific family". Australia's lack of such connections, and its size and power, mean it is difficult to argue for the same kind of special bond.

If Australia wants its "step-up" to yield results, improving the art of listening would be a good start

Because the Pacific islands have always occupied a central position in New Zealand foreign policy, its diplomats and officials tend to have a better understanding of island cultures, which has often helped to make their diplomacy more effective. New Zealand's more open approach to migration from Pacific island countries and its early adoption of a labour mobility scheme have helped endear island peoples to New Zealand. New Zealand prime ministers have also prioritised participation in the annual Pacific Islands Forum Leaders' Summit, while Australian prime ministers have regularly missed these meetings, leaving Pacific leaders to draw the obvious conclusion that the forum is not as important to Australia as APEC or ASEAN.

Wellington has distanced itself from the detention centres on Manus and Nauru, which has made it easier for it to manage relations with Port Moresby and Nauru. It has made efforts to ease the burden on these governments by offering to resettle some of the refugees – only to be repeatedly spurned by Canberra.

New Zealand has also diverged from Australia in increasing spending on broadcasting in the Pacific. Australia has cut spending on this crucial element of public diplomacy. The ABC has terminated its shortwave radio service to the region – and its frequencies have been taken over by the Chinese state broadcaster.

Prime Minister Jacinda Ardern has demonstrated a much greater understanding of climate change anxieties than her Australian counterpart. In a speech to the World Economic Forum in Davos in January 2019, Ardern said that climate change was the greatest threat facing the world and warned her fellow leaders not to find themselves on the wrong side of history. Ardern invoked the Pacific islands in her appeal to other world leaders: "It only takes a trip to the Pacific to see that climate change isn't … hypothetical, and you don't have to know anything about the science … to have someone from the Pacific island nations take you to a place they used to play as a child on the coast and show you where they used to stand and where the water now rises."

Even though Australian and New Zealand policy approaches in the Pacific are broadly similar, New Zealand projects a perception that it understands the region better than Australia does. It can do this because New Zealand ministers have traditionally visited the region more frequently than Australian ministers and are known for spending more time sitting down with Pacific island counterparts and hearing them out.

Jacinda Ardern speaks with evident compassion about the climate threat to the region while Australian ministers, including the current and former prime minister, are famous for joking about it. If Australia wants its "step-up" in the region to yield diplomatic results, improving the art of listening and demonstrating some empathy would be a good start.

China anxieties

The expanding influence of China in the Pacific islands has, over the last five years, begun to dent Australia's confidence about its ability to maintain dominance in the region. China's trade, investment and aid has grown at the same time as Australia's position on climate change has eroded the trust of Pacific island governments. China has become the region's second-largest trading partner after Australia, and is now its second-largest aid donor. While China contributed about $1.6 billion in aid between 2011 and 2017, this was still far behind Australia's spend of $8.7 billion over the same period; but the rapid rise in the volume and spread of Chinese aid, and China's willingness to fund projects that Australia will not, has meant that Pacific islands, with a broader choice of aid partners, no longer need to depend on Australia.

China is generally well regarded in Pacific island countries. The visibility of recent Chinese-funded infrastructure projects has created a perception that China understands what Pacific countries need and is quick to deliver. Fears about the negative impact of Chinese debt have not come to fruition (although Tonga is highly exposed in its debt). Chinese soft power, reflected through initiatives such as a regional tour by the People's Liberation Navy hospital ship *Daishan Dao*, also known as the Peace Ark, and through Chinese news services and training opportunities, has helped to portray an image of a benign benefactor. However, this image was challenged by the Chinese government's arrogant handling of the local media's access to events during Xi Jinping's visit to Papua New Guinea for APEC and by the disrespectful behaviour of Chinese foreign ministry officials at a meeting with Pacific Islands Forum Leaders in Nauru in 2018. There are concerns about Chinese labour being preferred for infrastructure projects and about Chinese migration to some Pacific island states. But most countries in the region believe that building a strong relationship with China will be good for their economies.

Anxiety about China's influence in Pacific island countries has served to sharpen Australia's focus on the region. Australia has pressured the British, French and US governments to expand their diplomatic presence in the region as a means of countering Chinese influence, and is building undersea internet cables to deny Huawei access. The prime ministers of Vanuatu, Solomon Islands and Papua New Guinea were all invited to Canberra in 2018 in a rushed show of amity. Scott Morrison visited Papua New Guinea, Vanuatu, Fiji and Solomon Islands within a period of seven months – an unprecedented run for an Australian prime minister. The government has signed bilateral security agreements with Solomon Islands, Nauru and Tuvalu, and is negotiating an agreement with Vanuatu.

China's show of power during President Xi Jinping's visit to the APEC Leaders' Summit in November 2018 created further apprehension in Canberra. If China follows through on ambitious Belt and Road infrastructure projects in Papua New Guinea, it could overtake the dollar value of Australia's aid contribution for the first time. Canberra's announcements about the establishment of a naval base in Manus; the building and management, with Fiji, of an Australian Pacific Security College in Fiji; and $250 million for a new Solomon Islands infrastructure fund signal to China that Australia is not willing to cede its regional position yet.

Pacific island officials will be looking to Canberra to support their lobbying on climate action

If faced with a hard choice on a strategic partner, most, if not all, Pacific island countries would likely back Australia over China. But most do not believe they will have to choose, and are confident

they can manage, as Australia does, having a primary economic partner that is not their primary security partner.

Domestic policy versus foreign policy

Australia has introduced new policies beyond security initiatives to
deliver benefits to Pacific island populations, but Canberra has poor
form on joining up its domestic and foreign policy initiatives. The
benefits of providing opportunities to Pacific islanders to work in
horticulture, tourism and hospitality is diminished so long as
Australia continues to extend visas for European and American
backpackers if they work in these same fields. Most employers find it
cheaper to use backpackers and are thus not incentivised to turn to
Pacific island workers.

At the Pacific Islands Forum in Nauru, Australia signed on
to the Boe Declaration, which asserted that climate change was the
"single greatest threat to the livelihoods, security and wellbeing of
the peoples of the Pacific" and pledged "commitment to progress the
implementation of the Paris Agreement". It was the first time Australia
had not had its way on climate change in the forum's communiqués.
But there was no suggestion in Canberra that this concession had consequences for domestic policy.

Scott Morrison's visits to Vanuatu and Fiji in January 2019 were
significant. This was the first time an Australian prime minister had
visited either country, outside of attending Pacific Islands Forum
meetings. Morrison's use, in a speech given in Suva, of the Fijian word

vuvale (family) to describe a different kind of Australian relationship with Pacific island countries – one that extends beyond diplomacy – introduced a concept that may help recalibrate Australia's standing in the region. Making his first post-election overseas visit to Solomon Islands is a further positive move in enhancing Australia's image. Whether Australia can adjust its domestic policy settings to accommodate this new kind of relationship, however, remains to be seen.

Measuring success

The success of Australia's step-up in the Pacific will be measured by different actors in different ways. The Australian prime minister and the defence and security establishment will be seeking evidence of a halt the growth of China's influence in the region. Pacific island leaders will be looking for a sustained closer relationship with Prime Minister Morrison and his key ministers. Pacific island officials will be looking to Canberra to develop an energy policy that reflects an awareness of the existential threat that climate change poses and to support their lobbying efforts on climate action in international forums.

Australian diplomats will be working to ensure Australia is the partner of choice for Pacific island countries on key projects in the future, preferred over China, and will be touting the benefits of the Australian Infrastructure Financing Facility for the Pacific. Pacific island communities will want to see Australian aid provide more direct and immediate benefits, rather than vague promises of a secure and prosperous future.

Scott Morrison's appointment of Alex Hawke as both Assistant Minister for Defence and Minister for International Development and the Pacific is an indication that the prime minister believes Australia's national security extends across the Pacific islands region. But securing the region is not only about strategic denial and increasing aid. The combination of responsibilities Hawke holds could be highly effective in pursuing Australia's interests – if the government acknowledges that climate change poses a grave security risk not only to Pacific states but also to Australia and the rest of the world. An assistant defence minister who is comfortable talking about climate change as a threat to security and who can mobilise more Australian and international assistance for mitigation, adaptation and resilience will win friends and trust in the Pacific. The Australian government could then build on that trust to have more serious conversations with island leaders about how the region can manage the growing influence of China – conversations that involve listening to leaders' concerns and sharing Australian evidence of the adverse impacts of Xi Jinping's foreign policy.

Without a radical new global approach to handling the climate emergency, the Pacific islands will never be secure – and Australia and the region will be dealing with a crisis more dangerous than the threat from Beijing. ■

NO DISTANT FUTURE

Climate change as
an existential threat

Katerina Teaiwa

The office of Nei Tabera Ni Kai (NTK), a film unit based in the town of Bairiki, in the small island nation of Kiribati, is a small concrete building situated two metres above sea level, thirty metres from the lagoon on one side and forty-five metres from the ocean on the other. Stacked under the louvered glass windows of one of its small rooms are 200 internal hard drives taken from computers over a period of twenty years. The office has no air conditioning, and the air is salty; there are regular electricity blackouts; and higher than normal wave surges, or "king tides", threaten the town – and the whole southern end of the atoll, South Tarawa, on which it is located – more frequently than they used to.

Once a Kiribati household name, NTK has not worked on major projects for a couple of years. One of the co-founders, John Anderson, cameraman and editor, passed away in 2016. His long-time partner, producer, manager and scriptwriter Linda Uan, has been dealing with the loss and reflecting on the best way to preserve their shared legacy. The independent film unit documented more than two decades of culture, history, creative arts practice, development, and social, heritage and environmental issues across the islands. In the absence of a national film agency or television media, NTK managed to piece together various sources of funding to work with government and communities to produce educational documentaries, feature films and "edutainment". Their output had a significant impact on the scattered Kiribati population – people from other islands travelled to South Tarawa by boat or canoe just to pick up the latest VHS, and later DVD, of their productions.

In March 2019, Uan attended the Maoriland Film Festival in Ōtaki, New Zealand, as part of a research project on Pacific women in film at Victoria University of Wellington. During a discussion panel, she spoke passionately about NTK's work over the years. She ended with a humble request for assistance with archiving, taking one of those rectangular hard drives containing raw footage from her handbag and unwrapping it from a *lavalava* (sarong), then holding it up for the audience to see. The group of New Zealand and international filmmakers gasped at the condition of the drive, and the prospective loss of decades of visual chronicles, exposed to the elements in Kiribati.

All but one of the thirty-three islands in Kiribati are less than two metres above sea level. Large parts of the country are expected to be underwater by 2050. From 2003 to 2016 Kiribati was led by President Anote Tong, who successfully raised global awareness of the climate change threats faced by his country. At the United Nations Climate Change Conference in Bonn in 2017, Kiribati was described as one of the world's most vulnerable countries. Annual temperatures in South Tarawa have increased by roughly 0.18 degrees Celsius per decade since 1950, according to the conference's briefing paper. This warming, coupled with increasingly ferocious tidal storms and coastal flooding, is destroying the island's ecosystems. Saltwater that floods the islands from storm surges devastates land and property, polluting reservoirs that capture and filter groundwater for consumption. Saltwater also jeopardises resources such as coconuts, pandanus and breadfruit, which residents rely on for food and many other household needs.

Cultural heritage and knowledge also face destruction due to climate change

The iconic giant swamp taro, or *babai*, is particularly sensitive to saltwater intrusion. In the Kiribati population, there has been a rise in waterborne diseases, among other climate-change-induced illnesses, including cholera and dengue fever.

Warming oceans, combined with increased ocean acidification, disrupts sea life, which is the cornerstone of Kiribati identity and the country's economy. The acidification is caused by carbon dioxide dissolving in the water. Due to the burning of fossil fuels, this is occurring ten times faster than it has during the past 300 million years. It threatens the biodiversity of the whole oceanic system. Kiribati depends almost entirely on its fishing sector for food and revenue, but the catch potential is expected to decrease by 70 per cent by the 2050s.

Kiribati is one of forty-eight nations in the Climate Vulnerable Forum, a partnership of countries most under threat from global warming. These include Tuvalu, Palau, Papua New Guinea, Fiji, Vanuatu, Samoa and the Marshall Islands. Kiribati once chaired the forum, and under Tong was a vocal proponent for limiting the temperature rise from global warming to 1.5 degrees Celsius. Beyond this temperature, sea levels are expected to increase to a point that would make Kiribati uninhabitable. Despite global campaigns calling for "1.5 to stay alive", the Paris Agreement on Climate Change seeks to limit the temperature rise to 2 degrees Celsius. This is devastating for most Pacific island countries.

Anote Tong was vocal about the need for Kiribati to face climate-induced migration "with dignity". However, the current government, led by Taneti Mamau, rejects this vision of mass migration, instead emphasising local development. The government aims to develop and increase the land area on South Tarawa by about 100 acres, and on Kiritimati (also known as Christmas Island) by 767 acres. It also owns 22 square kilometres of land on Vanua Levu in Fiji, with potential for forestry, livestock farming and other activities to shore up its food and economic security as Kiribati farmland comes under threat. Kiribati residents continue to do what they can on the ground. The Kiribati Climate Action Network, a largely female-led umbrella group for about fifty community-based organisations, works to address issues not only around climate change but also water management, sanitation, pollution, solar energy and mangrove nutrition, while assisting its members to participate in national and international climate discussions.

In recent years there has been a rapid expansion of climate-change research, journalism and field schools, and scientific adaption and mitigation programs, across Kiribati and other Pacific islands. Few of these consider the precarious status of cultural heritage and knowledge, which, like lands, livelihoods, food and water systems, and built environments, also face the threat of destruction due to climate change. International teams attempt to harness indigenous knowledge to better roll out their programs, but they rarely see the indigenous knowledge and cultures themselves as in need of safe-guarding. These are the kind of local practices, traditions and experiences – critical dimensions of island resilience – that Uan and Anderson captured on film. A Pacific song or dance is rarely only an empty form of entertainment – a dance and its accompanying chant may contain centuries of corporeal, social and environmental knowledge reflecting the need for balance between human societies and their natural environments. There is a rich chronicle of this in Kiribati, but its survival is not guaranteed.

Small islands, global leadership

While low-lying islands are not the only places in the world experiencing ecological stress and strain, Pacific leaders have been incredibly proactive in the international sphere in raising the urgent challenges their islands face. They use a range of tools, from formal diplomatic discussions and negotiations to films and cultural performances.

The Pacific has been inhabited for thousands of years. Before there were formal nations, islanders travelled the seas, forming strong kinship bonds and trade networks, and exchanging ideas and methods for resilience that have persisted beyond colonial divides. Scholars have tracked the spread of Austronesian languages across the region, as well as the movement of artistic styles, and pottery and obsidian left behind by cultures that were highly mobile and interconnected. When formal states were established in the late twentieth century and Pacific peoples achieved independence or self-governance, they were still able to harness those pre-colonial kinships, and created new regional networks to amplify their voices and priorities. One of these was the Festival of Pacific Arts, established in 1970 to help guard against the loss of identity and heritage. The festival runs every four years and brings together more than twenty-two countries and states to reaffirm the value of their cultural heritage, and to reinforce the relationship between this heritage and the oceans. Pacific international leadership on climate grows from this consistent care for Pacific communities and islands, and builds on decades of solidarity and action on other shared concerns, such as colonialism, mining and nuclear testing.

In 1991 the Pacific Islands Forum (then known as the South Pacific Forum) released a communiqué after its meeting in Palikir,

Pohnpei, in the Federated States of Micronesia, calling for "significant and immediate reductions" of greenhouse gases and pointing to the responsibility of industrialised countries to mitigate change in the climate. The communiqué stated, "Global warming and sea-level rise were the most serious environmental threats to the Pacific region. The cultural, economic and physical survival of Pacific nations was at great risk." The forum recognised that stabilising greenhouse-gas emissions would require greater energy efficiency and alternative energy sources and technologies.

It called upon all countries, particularly industrialised countries, to prioritise research, development and the transfer of technologies in these areas.

Small Pacific islands are condescendingly seen as vulnerable, always in need of aid

These statements reflected the position of the Alliance of Small Island States (AOSIS), a grouping of fifteen Pacific countries established in 1990 to address global warming. The alliance helped design the 1992 UN Framework Convention on Climate Change, ensuring it addressed the specific concerns of small island countries. Working together, states that were regularly sidelined in global arenas began to assert their agency, managing to ensure their interests were incorporated into a historic international convention.

In a lecture at the Australian National University in 2013, the former Nauru ambassador to the United Nations, Marlene Moses, reminded her Australian audience of this leadership. She said, "Early on, AOSIS earned [a] reputation for advocating for policies that are rigorously based in science and calculated to reduce emissions to a level that is consistent with the survival of all our members." She recalled that the first UN proposal calling for a multilateral approach to tackling global warming, what would eventually become the Kyoto Protocol, was drafted by Nauru and submitted under the chairmanship of Trinidad and Tobago in 1994. Such leadership is at odds with the popular perception of small Pacific islands, in which they are condescendingly seen as vulnerable or underdeveloped, always in need of advice and aid from larger metropolitan countries. The Australian media, and certain activists, scholars, policymakers and leaders, often present Pacific nations as corrupt or conflict-prone "failed states", whose instability is viewed in simplistic and often racialised terms. The discussion tends to be paternalistic and narrowly focused on development and security, with little concern for equity or social stability. Knowledge of the region's historical and cultural contexts remains shallow.

Australian flippancy

The prevailing Australian discourse on the Pacific, which frames the region as either a paradise or a site of crisis, is decades old, but flourished particularly just before and after John Howard became prime minister in 1996. Pacific agency and efficacy were often ignored or presumed non-existent. Images of fatalism were regularly conjured, as the Australian National University scholar Greg Fry argued, within "the intersecting worlds of the Australian bureaucrat, the politician, the foreign affairs journalist, and the academic economist". Analogies and metaphors abounded, with the South Pacific seen as either the hole in the "Asia-Pacific doughnut" or the eye of the "Asia-Pacific cyclone", precursors to the Melanesian-centred post-9/11 "Arc of Instability" or "Arc of Crisis".

Fry's argument was made in response to a 1993 Australian National University Pacific Futures project in which journalist Rowan Callick sketched a powerful scenario of a "Pacific doomsday", predicting that the region would be beset by 2010 with out-of-control population growth, widespread malnutrition, high levels of poverty, degraded lands and environments, pollution, major skills shortages and crime. Rather than seeing these trends as the result of the colonial transformation of previously sustainable cultures, or of colonial resource extraction, or, indeed, of pollution and demands for Pacific resources from industrial countries, Callick attributed the problem to Pacific economies' failures to implement structural adjustment – to support financial competition, corporatisation and privatisation. For successive journalists, analysts and Australian governments, including the Morrison government, free trade, rather than the climate action strategies islanders themselves are calling for, is the answer to the Pacific's problems.

Despite significant developments since 1993 – increases in tourism, numerous AusAID programs, Julie Bishop's "aid-for-trade" measures, the New Colombo Plan, a reimagining of part of the region as an "Indo-Pacific", and Scott Morrison's recent Pacific "step-up" – not much has changed in Australian attitudes towards the islands. A few months ago a former Minister for the Environment, Melissa Price, was introduced to Anote Tong in a Canberra restaurant during a dinner hosted by Labor senator Pat Dodson. The senator had visited Kiribati in 2010 as part of a program organised by the Edmund Rice Centre to forge deeper links between Indigenous Australians and Pacific Islanders. Upon Price's introduction to Tong, an internationally respected statesman, it was widely reported – and verified by others in the restaurant – that she said, "I know why you're here. It is for the cash. For the Pacific it's always about the cash. I have my chequebook here. How much do you want?"

Price's comments were likely inspired by her observations of how other members of the Coalition characterised the Pacific. Liberal Queensland senator Ian Macdonald had earlier accused Pacific nations of "swindling money from Australia to address the effects of rising sea levels". *The Sydney Morning Herald* reported him as saying, "They might be Pacific islanders, but there's no doubting their wisdom and their ability to extract a dollar where they see it." In a similar vein was Peter Dutton's flippant aside in 2015 in response to a quip by Tony Abbott about how islanders are not good at keeping to time. Dutton said, "Time doesn't mean anything when you're about to have water lapping at your door."

Macdonald's comments followed the urgent climate action priorities set at the Pacific Islands Forum meeting on Nauru in 2018.

The head of the Pacific Islands Forum, Dame Meg Taylor, gave a speech at the Australian National University in which she said that climate change had brought "truly desperate times" to the region and that "it is absolutely essential that we work together to move the discussion with Australia to develop a pathway that will minimise the impacts of climate change for the future of all ... including Australia."

For months this plea was ignored, but in the lead-up to the federal election in May 2019, action on climate change appeared to be a priority for a large section of the Australian population, particularly young people. Of the two major parties, Labor had the more-ambitious climate plan, but social and mainstream media was filled with discussion about

These days, Pacific island countries are not always feeling friendly towards Australia

the economic implications. In the end, the expectation of a climate change–driven election was not met. The perceived threat to individual pockets of society and to jobs in coalmining regions outweighed the threat to the planet. Australians voted for the status quo.

The level of carbon now in the atmosphere is more than 415 parts per million. The last time the Earth experienced these levels was during the Pliocene Epoch, between 5.3 and 2.5 million years ago. Then, global temperatures were 2 to 3 degrees Celsius higher, and the sea levels 25 metres higher. Pollution from climate change today is on track to push the Earth towards similar conditions. To many voters, this reality is too much to fathom, presumed to be a hoax, or utterly unknown. Scott Morrison might support climate adaptation and mitigation programs in the Pacific through his "Pacific step-up", but he does not support similar domestic policies, such as increased research on climate change or the introduction of a carbon price, and Australia has no renewable energy targets beyond 2030. It is the world's second-largest exporter of coal but faces falling demand as its biggest customers – Japan, South Korea, China, Taiwan and India – all shift towards cleaner energy. Burning coal is in Australia a bit like the right to bear arms in the United States: a freedom that causes major planetary harm, but the issue is severely politicised and many are not willing to imagine a future without it.

This protection of the mining industry is not new. For more than a century Australia has had a relationship with the South Pacific region that furthered its economic interests. Australian mining companies have been present in the Pacific since the beginning of the twentieth century, wreaking havoc on ancient cultures and sustainable environmental practices while extracting phosphate as quickly as possible from places such as Nauru and Kiribati. Australian agriculture thrived while destroying the landscapes of much smaller Pacific islands. The value of phosphate, the superphosphate fertiliser it produced, and the growth effects it had on Australian farming production and exports were massive. In 1983 a monograph produced by the Centre for Resource and Environmental Studies described phosphate as "the magic dust of Australian agriculture". Phosphate drove a whole system of Australian prosperity and development, and much of it came from nations in the Pacific that are today accused of making grabs for cash. These islands weren't rehabilitated, and in the case of Banaba, an island that forms part of Kiribati, the mining infrastructure was left to rust and decay. People there live among the asbestos-riddled rubble, in a place that looks more like a post-apocalyptic lunarscape than a Pacific paradise. Banaba's closest neighbour, Nauru, is now one of the most vilified places in the world because of Australia's offshore detention centres, but prior to mining initiated by Australia, New Zealand and the United Kingdom, the Europeans called it "Pleasant Island" because its people were so friendly to outsiders.

These days, Pacific island countries are not always feeling friendly towards Australia. At the 2018 Forum meeting, Nauru president Baron Waqa and a group of elders made a point of singling out New Zealand prime minister Jacinda Arden for special honour and friendship – not Australia, represented by Minister for Foreign Affairs Marise Payne. They sang Ardern an original composition titled "Jacinda, New Star in the Sky", celebrating her leadership and the birth of her daughter. Waqa himself played the guitar.

What kinds of policies and attitudes have converted generally friendly islanders into what Australian leaders today think of as thankless cash-grabbers? The disdain and constant-deficit view of the Pacific promoted by more than a few Australian "Pacific experts" is underpinned by public ignorance of the region and its people.

When Peter Dutton made his offensive comment in 2015, Tony deBrum, the former foreign minister for the Marshall Islands, posted on Twitter, "Next time waves are battering my home & my grandkids are scared, I'll ask Peter Dutton to come over, and we'll see if he is still laughing." Price's words to Tong were also offensive. That kind of attitude towards Pacific island leaders needs to change. Such leaders have been criticising the production and consumption of fossil fuels and their impacts on the environment for almost thirty years. Marlene Moses wrote in 2016, "For the people of small islands, understanding the importance of the ocean to human survival is as natural as breathing. If the ocean is healthy, we are healthy; if the future of the ocean is uncertain, so is ours." The Pacific islands may be smaller states demographically and geographically, but the sea in which they sit covers one-third of the planet's surface area. Pacific leadership on climate change is necessary and inevitable.

How to address the climate call

Visions of water lapping at the door do not seem to translate into concern about Australia's fossil-fuel contributions. Per capita, Australia is one of the world's highest fossil-fuel emitters, but there is a counternarrative presented across conservative media that focuses on Australia's proportion of total global emissions. Commentator Alan Jones compared Australia's contribution – 1.3 per cent of all emissions – to a grain of rice in a 1.75-kilogram bag of rice. The argument was that nothing Australia could do to reduce its fossil-fuel footprint would make a difference globally. Charlie Pickering, on ABC news comedy show *The Weekly*, countered with a different analogy: "Yes, we're just one grain of rice, but we've always been just one grain of rice. In World War Two we made up just 2 per cent of the Western Allies fighting overseas, but we didn't decide not to fight because we were too small to make a difference. We took pride in doing our part because the consequences of doing nothing were unthinkable." On the international stage, Australia often plays a role that is disproportionately larger than its population. It is the world's thirteenth-largest economy, has the thirteenth-largest military expenditure, and has sufficient diplomatic clout to have effectively led the push for international responses

Climate change may be an existential threat, but "vulnerable" does not mean "incapable"

on issues such as trans-Pacific free trade, multinational tax avoidance, and regulation of social media companies.

So what should Australia do to play its part in reducing this existential threat? Globally, human societies and the industries that support our lifestyles put 38.2 billion tonnes of carbon dioxide into the atmosphere each year. Temperatures are likely to reach 1.5 degrees Celsius above pre-industrial levels between 2030 and 2052 if emissions continue to increase at the current rate. Australia's Pacific "step-up", described in 2018 by Marise Payne as a foreign policy imperative, outlines a range of economic, security and relationship-building plans.

The Department of Foreign Affairs and Trade says that the "step-up" responds to the "significant long-term challenges faced by our partners in the Pacific, including climate change and responding to natural disasters". Given the resounding election win by the coal-friendly Coalition, this pledge to support challenges related to climate change in the islands does not appear to translate into action at home.

After the Australian federal election, Fiji prime minister Frank Bainimarama, who appears fairly positive about Australia–Fiji relations, congratulated Scott Morrison and urged him to be a good "earthly steward" of Australia. President Hilda Heine of the Marshall Islands is less optimistic. After the Australian federal budget in April 2019 confirmed that Australia would no longer contribute to the Green Climate Fund, which helps developing countries fight the climate crisis, she wrote on Twitter, "We look to our regional partners for leadership & solidarity. Not this."

Former prime minister Kevin Rudd proposed in a February 2019 essay, "The Complacent Country", that Pacific islanders swap their climate-threatened lands for Australian citizenship and Australian control over Pacific maritime resources. He did not contend with the deep connection that Pacific islanders have to their ancestral lands and their willingness to defend and protect the places that have given them thousands of years of sustenance, heritage, identity, creativity and survival skills. The Tuvaluan prime minister, Enele Sopoaga, described Rudd's proposal for Nauru, Kiribati and Tuvalu as a form of "neo-colonialism", especially in light of the $66 billion in Australian coal exports in 2018. "The days of that type of imperial thinking are over," Sopoaga told the ABC. "The [climate change] cause is not only about small island countries, it is everybody's cause, everybody's safety and security of living on this planet – there is no Plan B."

There are many things that Australia should do to address the climate action calls from its Pacific neighbours. First, it can check the language of all official programs and partnerships and ask if they have a neo-colonialist or patronising tone. Do they presume a lack of capacity, or will they seek out and draw on the skill and resilience inherent in Pacific populations? At the federal level, Australian policymakers also need to realise that the Pacific isn't just out there in the islands. It's in Australian cities, with growing numbers of Pacific migrants and descendants of South Sea Islanders. Those numbers will increase with rising tides of seasonal workers and scholarships for Pacific high-school students to study in Australian schools. Many young Australians with ancestral connections to the Pacific islands care about climate change and participate in protest and discussions about the issue. Experts, stakeholders and advocates with great ideas for adaptation, mitigation and resilience are right here, in Australian cities, studying at Australian universities. Climate change may be an existential threat, but "vulnerable" does not mean "incapable".

Second, Australia can heed the calls of young Australians, Torres Strait Islanders, natural and social scientists, Pacific island communities, and Pacific island and global leaders, and question the true impact of existing and proposed new coalmines and coal-fired power stations. On a recent trip to the region, UN chief António Guterres called for a halt to coal-fired power stations and for a turn from "a grey to a green economy". Given the election results and Scott Morrison's famous defence of a lump of coal in the Australian parliament, it seems unlikely that this government will do what it must and consider economically inspiring alternatives, plus plan for those who work in mining and fossil-fuel-related industries to be transitioned into renewable energy or similar sectors. The government will have to consider the kinds of communication and awareness programs needed to convince Australians this is possible.

The extreme politicisation of the climate change debate in Australia has ended several political careers. With no meaningful domestic energy policy and no Department of Climate Change to coalesce the concerns of business, defence, development, health, environment, security and other stakeholders, it will be very difficult for Australia to play its role in the international race to reduce carbon emissions. Australian politics does not align with Australian science or Australian policy advice. This country has all the resources, technology, evidence and information it needs to act on climate change. For the sake of everyone, including those in the Pacific islands, it just needs the political will and leadership.

Thirdly, Pacific Studies are sorely needed across the country at every level of education. Australia is located in the Pacific, too. The history, geography and knowledge of Melanesian, Micronesian and Polynesian cultures and societies should be integrated into

Australian primary, high-school and tertiary curriculums. This would help to explain and provide context for the $1.4 billion in Australian development assistance projected for 2019–2020 for the Pacific. And it would combat the ignorance that has led to misguided policies and diplomacy by successive Australian governments and to regrettable statements by some of its MPs.

Since 1997, Nei Tabera Ni Kai has produced more than 400 films in both English and the Kiribati language focused on Kiribati knowledge, lives, issues and communities. They have documented what residents call *"te katei ni Kiribati"* – the Kiribati way. Their work should be stored in a well-funded archive and maintained for posterity. The name of the unit comes from a female ancestral spirit belonging to Linda Uan's clan, responsible for women's health and success. Climate change threatens not only the lands of families and clans such as hers, but the spiritual and cultural spheres associated with these landscapes. The knowledge inherent in these spheres has been the source of resilience for more than 2000 years in an oceanic environment with limited land, flora and fauna, allowing islanders not only to survive but to produce complex, creative societies.

Climate change is here today, not just in some distant future

Australia is now saturated with messages about the existential threat of climate change, but the impacts will cut across all dimensions of human existence – the social, the political, the cultural, the economic, the environmental, and everything else that shapes our identities and relationships. Climate change is here today, not just in some distant future, and Pacific islanders who cannot always crawl into air-conditioned, climate-controlled bubbles experience its effects on a daily basis. While the people of the Pacific are resilient and have survived centuries of upheaval, climate change is already at emergency levels in the region – representing some of the first and starkest signs of the greatest ecological threat to ever face humanity. ■

THE PAPUA NEW GUINEA AWAKENING

Inside the forgotten colony

Sean Dorney

Between 1974 and 1999, I spent twenty years as a journalist in Papua New Guinea. Following that, I spent fifteen years reporting on and from the Pacific islands, with a visit or two back to Papua New Guinea each year. Unfortunately, not long after the ABC made me redundant in 2014, I was diagnosed with motor neurone disease. It has severely limited my ability to type. Whereas once I was a ten-fingered typist, I am now down to two fingers, and even that is laboured. For my recent birthday, my wife, Pauline, and my two children bought me Dragon voice-recognition software. I could not have written this essay without it. But it is not perfect – especially with unfamiliar words.

I have been transcribing the extensive notes that my late mother wrote in longhand on our family history. In the mid-1970s,

I spent three years on secondment from the ABC to the newly created National Broadcasting Commission of Papua New Guinea. My mother wrote about how, in 1975, she and my father came to Port Moresby to watch me play as a halfback for the national rugby league team, the Kumuls. Dragon made a stab at autocorrect. "Kumul" is the Melanesian Pidgin word for "bird of paradise". However, according to Dragon, the national rugby league team is not named "the Kumuls" but "the Criminals".

That software quirk amused me, but it also annoyed me on a number of levels. Given the limited and often one-dimensional coverage of Papua New Guinea we get today in the Australian media, many Australians could probably be forgiven for believing that "the Criminals" may be an apt name for any group representing Papua New Guinea. Yet it is far from true. Crime is almost non-existent in my wife's village of Koropalek, on Manus Island, where the people live a predominantly subsistence lifestyle – feeding themselves from their gardens and the sea, and beating sago.

It is not only the Australian media that gives Papua New Guinea a bad rap. The BBC ran an article last year claiming that 70 per cent of Papua New Guinean women can expect to be raped at some stage in their life. Over the years, I have met and worked with a significant number of Papua New Guinean women, and spent weeks at a time living in my wife's village. Unless the sample of women I know is completely unrepresentative, that figure is a ridiculous exaggeration. Rape is definitely a problem in the congested cities and towns, as is gender violence. But some 80 per cent of Papua New Guineans still live in villages, and rape is so socially destructive that, in the village setting, it would be met with immediate retribution. Last year, the ABC sent a camera team with Pauline and me to her village on Manus. During our visit, we produced two programs – a half-hour *Foreign Correspondent* and a forty-five-minute documentary for the ABC News channel. Pauline and I are often stopped by people when we are out shopping in Brisbane, where we live, and the most common comment is how healthy and joyful the people in her village are.

Australians' understanding of what is happening in Papua New Guinea has narrowed dramatically

Papua New Guinea is still struggling with governance, it's true. This is due to how rapidly it has moved from more than 1000 tiny, subsistence nation-states to a single country. Its eight to nine million people speak 860 distinct languages. For instance, in the Nuku District, just inland from Aitape, in the West Sepik Province, the people speak at least thirty-seven languages. It's no wonder the biblical story of the Tower of Babel resonates so strongly in the nation. (Christian churches are hugely important to the population, and health and education services would be much poorer without the hospitals, aid clinics and schools funded and run by church agencies. Both the Catholic Church and the Seventh-day Adventists operate universities in Papua New Guinea, one in Madang and one in Port Moresby.)

Australia administered Papua for more than seventy years, and New Guinea for well over fifty – we took over New Guinea following World War I, after Australian prime minister Billy Hughes demanded at the Versailles Peace Conference that Australia be given control of what had been German New Guinea. But we did not administer the two territories as one colony until after World War II. Despite the tremendous work of Australian patrol officers and others, Papua New Guinea was far from a cohesive whole when independence came in 1975. As late as 1970 – just five years before independence – an area of some 170,000 hectares was still classified as not under administrative control. The Highlands were not discovered by the outside world until the 1930s, and it was not until the 1950s and 1960s that many in the Highlands came into contact with outsiders. Given that history, it is intriguing how little we know these days about what is going on inside this former colony of ours.

The price of ignorance

Australians' understanding of what is happening in Papua New Guinea has narrowed dramatically over the past forty-four years. Back in 1975, when I was working for the National Broadcasting Commission, there were six Australian journalists based in Port Moresby, covering events throughout the country for the media back home. There were two in the ABC bureau; one each for the Australian Associated Press (AAP), Fairfax, and the Herald and Weekly Times; and one freelancer earning a decent living reporting for a number of other Australian news outlets. When Papua New Guinea did not immediately falter as a nation, the Australian media lost interest. It is not cheap to maintain a correspondent in Port Moresby, and the various bureaus gradually closed down. By the mid-1980s, there were just two Australian journalists based in the city – one at the ABC and one at AAP. Several years ago, AAP also shut down its reporting from Port Moresby. Now, the ABC's Natalie Whiting struggles on alone.

Whiting is doing a great job but, as the solitary correspondent, she is the only reference point for those who decide what is run on the main news and current-affairs programs at the ABC. When I was the ABC correspondent, I would sometimes ensure that other journalists were aware of stories I regarded as significant. The simple reasoning was that if a story from Papua New Guinea featured in, for example, *The Sydney Morning Herald,* my version would almost certainly get a run on the ABC Radio current-affairs program *AM.* It was almost the opposite mindset to getting a scoop.

The reporting that emerges from Papua New Guinea is often significant for Australia, as demonstrated by two recent examples that highlight how much we potentially miss due to our poor coverage.

One poignant story that Whiting reported recently concerned children born from relationships between asylum seekers and local Manus women. "In a patch of jungle on Manus," Whiting began, "the two-year-old is happily passed between his mother and grandmother outside their humble hut, but his paler skin makes him stand out. He is one of up to forty children who have been fathered by asylum seekers and refugees on Manus Island. His mother, Flora Boyoeu, is no longer in a relationship with Christopher's father." Some asylum seekers have married and want to take their wives and children with them if they are resettled. But the fate of children born of relationships that have ended is uncertain. "A spokesperson for the Home Affairs department confirmed to the ABC," Whiting reported, "the children were covered under the Medevac Law and could be transferred to Australia as 'legacy minors'. How that would work, and under what conditions they would be transferred, remains unclear." And what about the mothers?

Although I have been critical of much of the Australian media's reporting on Papua New Guinea, an exception is the *Australian Financial Review*'s investigative reporting of the Paladin contract for Manus. This tiny Australian-owned company was awarded $423 million in security contracts by the Australian government in a closed tender. I can appreciate some of the complications in administering security on Manus – larger companies involved earlier in the tender process had decided it wasn't worth the fallout with institutional shareholders scared off by determined asylum-seeker advocacy. But $423 million! Maybe one of the problems is that very few officials in Canberra, who make these decisions, know much at all about Papua New Guinea. It's also disheartening when even one of Australia's best journalists, Paul Kelly, writes in *The Australian* that Indonesia's closest neighbour is Australia. Papua New Guinea claims that status; it shares a large land border with Indonesia. But Australia is so close to Papua New Guinea that three Australian islands in the Torres Strait have been excised from PNG's territorial seas. Australia's knowledge of our nearest neighbour is abysmal – and we are paying a price for our ignorance.

Thank goodness for China

Earlier this year, the Queensland chapter of the Australian Institute of International Affairs invited me to speak about Australia's sudden re-engagement with Papua New Guinea and the Pacific. I told them that I was tempted to use the title "Thank goodness for China!" If China had been less active in cultivating our Pacific neighbours, Canberra's atten-

Australian politicians have long regarded the Pacific as a "strategic backwater"

tion would never have refocused on what has rather embarrassingly been called "our patch".

Scott Morrison's "Pivot to the Pacific", announced last November, includes a $2 billion infrastructure bank for Pacific island nations, allowing them to access discounted loans for ports, roads and telecommunications infrastructure. Also under the plan, five new Australian diplomatic missions are to be opened in the Pacific, and the Australian government will ramp up military cooperation, with more navy deployments in the region and a permanent defence force team tasked with training their Pacific island counterparts.

Jonathan Pryke, my colleague at the Lowy Institute, agrees with me (and likely everybody who has thought about this sudden pivot) that such moves are all about China. In late 2018, he told ABC News journalist Stephen Dziedzic that most Australian politicians have long regarded the Pacific as a "strategic backwater". "Geopolitics in the Pacific had been pretty benign since World War II," he said, so Australia was "able to operate with a degree of benign neglect". But since 2006, China has gradually built up political influence across the region. The Chinese "are on the ground everywhere", according to Pryke, and "policymakers have finally taken note".

Before I departed the ABC, I saw many of the infrastructure projects funded mostly by Chinese loans: buildings, ports, roads. Pacific island politicians could proudly point to these shiny new developments as markers of progress. Australia's aid has traditionally been directed towards the supposedly loftier realms of health, education and governance. But I often heard the complaint that our assistance was "boomerang aid", with Australian consultants and companies pocketing a good proportion of the money.

The looming Pacific "debt trap" – the possibility that small Pacific nations will take on unsustainable loans that leave them indebted to Beijing – is a concern. But is our $2 billion infrastructure bank going to saddle Pacific nations with even more debt?

China's initial forays may involve aid and loans, but in various places that has been closely followed by major Chinese commercial investments. The governor of Port Moresby, Powes Parkop, who is a member of the national parliament, told Natalie Whiting that while China's increased involvement in the region may be a concern for Australia and the United States, it was not a concern for Papua New Guinea. An alliance with China was logical: "At the moment the Chinese are investing. It's not that we are bending over and saying, 'Just come and do whatever you want.' We're going through the process," he said.

There is speculation that China has ambitions to build a military base, or several, in the Pacific. Vanuatu has been mentioned as a possible location, but both the Chinese and the Vanuatu governments have scoffed at that. China's apparent interest in helping Papua New Guinea redevelop its naval base on Manus Island prompted a counter-offer from the United States and Australia. Governor Parkop was scathing about that recent announcement. "I'm particularly concerned about the US and Australian influence on us ... the naval facility in Manus, I don't think that's in PNG's interest. I think that's in their interest. If it was in PNG's interest and win-win, they should have done it a long time ago." Governor Parkop, who hails from Manus, claimed he raised the idea of redeveloping the base with Australia back in 2014 but it failed to attract interest. "Why now? The only reason now is because of China."

There is a perfect example of China's approach to investment in Papua New Guinea. A Chinese syndicate led by Baosen International Holding is about to spend $414 million building a Chinatown in Port Moresby. I know the land they have chosen quite well – it is not far from NBC Studios, where I worked in the mid-1970s, and the former site of various transmitters owned by the state's telecommunications body, PNG Telecom. In April, the first sod was turned on what has been described as the largest-ever Chinese investment in the nation: this Chinatown will include apartments, shops, restaurants, a cinema and a hotel. Whiting reported that some of Papua New Guinea's top politicians joined the Chinese ambassador and the developer at the ceremony.

But questions have been raised about how the Chinese syndicate acquired the Telecom land. An NBC television news reporter, Rose Amos, was stonewalled when she attempted to find an answer. The nation's Minister for Lands and Physical Planning, Justin Tkatchenko, said he did not know. "This was before my time ... I wouldn't have a clue. You'd have to ask them, the investor ... Ask the investor how much they paid." A representative of Boasen International Holding, Sen Lin, told her, "Sorry, that's confidential. The purchase is between company and company, so it's confidential. We can't disclose that." And Governor Parkop said he had no idea. "You would have to ask Telecom. I don't know. I wish I knew. It's a private matter for Telecom and I am not privy to it. I hope they got very good money, but if not, that is a problem that Telecom has to explain." The CEO of PNG Telecom said he had no knowledge of the financial outcome of the deal and referred Amos to a government-owned entity, Kumul Consolidated Holdings. It would not respond to her enquiries.

A few days after that sod-turning ceremony, Papua New Guinea's prime minister, Peter O'Neill, flew to China to represent the Pacific at a forum on China's global infrastructure program, the Belt and Road Initiative. The Chinese ambassador to Papua New Guinea, Xue Bing, wished him well on his trip to Beijing and commended the strengthening relationship. "In 2018, through the joint efforts of both sides, the bilateral trade volume between China and PNG increased by 27 per cent," Mr Xue said in his speech. "China's direct investment in PNG reached [$5.06 billion], also a big increase."

China's interest in Papua New Guinea – indeed, in the whole Pacific – is only going to grow, and with that comes growing influence.

China's interest in Papua New Guinea is only going to grow

Politics and patronage

Politics in Papua New Guinea has a history of volatility. Allegations of corruption abound, and several commissions of enquiry over the years have revealed significant problems. The expectation of the voters, and the often extraordinary demands constituents make on their MPs, would likely frighten any Australian politician.

Successful motions of no confidence were a regular feature of Papua New Guinea's first twenty-five years of self-government. Here's a quick potted history. Julius Chan brought down Michael Somare in parliament in 1980. Somare returned in the 1982 elections, but Paias Wingti brought him down midterm in 1985. Wingti formed government again after the 1987 election, but he fell to Rabbie Namaliu in a no-confidence vote in 1988. Wingti emerged from the 1992 elections leading the government, but Chan ousted him mid-term in 1994. Chan lost his seat in 1997, following the military's expulsion of the Sandline mercenaries that his government had contracted to try to wipe out the secessionist leaders in Bougainville. Bill Skate emerged from those 1997 elections as prime minister, but he lost to Mekere Morauta in a parliamentary vote in 1999.

Morauta helped to halt this merry-go-round: he passed the *Organic Law on the Integrity of Political Parties and Candidates*, introducing some constitutional amendments that have contributed to greater stability since. Before his recent demise, Peter O'Neill had survived as prime minister for eight years. During that time Australia had five prime ministers. But a flurry of defections in the past few months finally undid him, and he announced in late May that he would resign.

O'Neill had done much to shore up his position as prime minister by vastly increasing the amount of money flowing directly to members of parliament to be spent at their discretion, under a number of schemes, including what is known as the District Services Improvement Program. In 2016, these disbursements amounted to $15 million kina (PNG's local currency) to members each year. The current deputy prime minister, Charles Abel, cut these amounts by 80 per cent in a supplementary budget late in 2017. That did not please a lot of MPs.

In March 2019, after a considerable delay, the Australian National University released its report on its observation of Papua New

Guinea's 2017 elections. The 258-person observation team, funded by the university and the Australian Aid Program, comprised thirty-two Papua New Guinea academics or researchers, thirty-one ANU-based academics and students, 192 Papua New Guinea observers and three ANU support staff. It rather dwarfed the twelve-member-and-support-staff Commonwealth Observer Group of which I was part.

In launching the ANU report, Professor Betty Lovai, executive dean of the University of Papua New Guinea's School of Humanities and Social Sciences, reflected on her observations as team leader of the Moresby North West electorate – particularly on citizens' attitudes to the elections. "People of PNG recognise the importance of elections, there's no doubt about that ... It was demonstrated from my observation that people wanted to vote." However, Lovai also noted that there were a number of issues that prevented individuals from doing so. One issue that all the observer teams commented on was the dreadful state of the common roll. We members of the Commonwealth Observer Group found that in almost every electorate we covered, people were turned away because their names were not on the roll – many told us they had voted in the previous election, five years earlier. The electoral commissioner authorised the use of the 2012 common roll as a supplementary roll, but we found that many polling stations did not refer to it. It seemed to us that poor administration, rather than deliberate manipulation, was the source of the problem.

Sir Mekere Morauta, the member for Moresby North West, seized on the ANU report, and in a news release titled "O'Neill Government

Corruption", he accused "foreign governments" and observer missions – such as mine – of "whitewashing the rigging and corruption" associated with the election. He was particularly critical of the Australian Department of Foreign Affairs. "Most Papua New Guineans," Morauta said, "expect Australia not to tolerate corruption ... We were amazed and very disappointed that the Australian government not only seemed to condone what had happened but continued to praise Peter O'Neill publicly."

However, a sober look at the results reveals that this was no electoral triumph for O'Neill's People's National Congress party. In fact, while 55 per cent of all sitting members were defeated, O'Neill's party MPs fared worse than the rest. His PNC lost thirty-four sitting members, just over 60 per cent of those who faced the voters. That is hardly a successful effort at rigging the contest. But the PNC did win seven seats it did not hold before, and so wound up with twenty-eight – almost double the number of the second-largest party, the National Alliance. And, consequently, as provided for in the Constitution, O'Neill was invited to negotiate to form government.

Before being part of the observer team in 2017, I covered at least five elections in Papua New Guinea, and although they seem to have become increasingly shambolic, I have seen little evidence of massive organised corruption. On one point I agree with Morauta. He concluded his release, "The ANU report should be a wake-up call for Australia to start thinking more constructively about its engagement with Papua New Guinea." Closer engagement will not only improve ties between these two neighbours but will lead to a more informed debate in Australia about how to help Papua New Guinea resolve its many development challenges.

Making aid count

Australia's bilateral aid to Papua New Guinea will amount to $512 million in 2019–20. It has been in the vicinity of half a billion dollars a year for some time now – roughly double that given to Indonesia, Australia's second-largest recipient.

A crucial question, as Australia seeks to re-engage with Papua New Guinea, is: what can it do to make its aid more effective?

Papua New Guinea's deputy prime minister, Charles Abel,

We [must] increase our presence in and understanding of our nearest neighbour

suggests that Australian aid should have "education as its primary focus". In an address to the Lowy Institute in June last year, he advocated providing 500 to 1000 places annually in Australian boarding schools for Papua New Guinea's highest achievers, from Grade 9 on. He proposed placing Australian lecturers and teachers in Papua New Guinea's universities and schools, and vice versa. Abel predicted that "four or five hundred Papua New Guineans returning per year from the Australian high school or university system" was the fastest way "to create the critical mass of a middle class to feed into leadership, bureaucracy and business innovation".

Abel also proposed a modern ICT infrastructure network to improve global integration. A new 20-terabyte cable from Sydney to Port Moresby, currently under construction, and a domestic submarine cable and terrestrial fibre-optic network will be crucial for this. "Access to cheap, speedy internet means access to knowledge and education – it's a no-brainer," Abel contended. An educated population "is the key" because Papua New Guinea has "all the other elements necessary in the development equation".

Perhaps helping Papua New Guinea build a new hospital in Port Moresby should also be considered. Professor Glen Mola, the head of Obstetrics and Gynaecology at Port Moresby General Hospital, has drawn attention to the hospital's inability to cope with "the load of patients in just about every department". He said in a post on Facebook: "Last year we had over 14,000 births in our twenty-four-bed delivery suite. We do not have the space, we do not have the resources and we do not have the staff to look after all these women properly. Port Moresby is the only capital city in the world (of size more than half a million people) with only one public hospital. For our size we should have at least three large public hospitals and a number of functional district hospitals."

Port Moresby General Hospital is the national referral and teaching hospital, but Mola said it has to operate at the level of primary care. "We are swamped with thousands of women having essentially normal birth (but requiring careful observation for any obstetric or newborn emergency), and this often means that we do not have the space or the staff available to properly look after the very high risk and problematic and extremely dangerous pregnancies properly." In a direct appeal to politicians, and one that should also be heeded by Canberra, he continued: "Can the government please stop building prestige (look at me) projects, and put resources into the ordinary care facilities that ordinary people need every day please."

Time for an awakening

One only needs to be in Papua New Guinea on the night of a Queensland versus New South Wales State of Origin rugby league clash to understand how passionately Papua New Guineans regard the Australia–PNG relationship. When I was the ABC correspondent in Port Moresby, it never ceased to amaze me how a sporting event in another country could consume so many locals. The goodwill exists towards Australia from many on the Papua New Guinea side. It may have taken an increasing Chinese presence in the Pacific region to stir up some recognition in Canberra that Australia needs to do more to revitalise the relationship from our side. But whatever the motivation, that increased focus is more than welcome.

The challenge now is to ensure that this attention is maintained, and that we increase our presence in and understanding of our nearest neighbour. Papua New Guinea is complex and has, over the past forty-four years, been prone to Australian neglect and misunderstanding. But this occurs to our peril and our shame, and to the benefit of other regional players and competitors. ∎

THE FIX *Solving Australia's foreign affairs challenges*
—

Euan Graham on How to Plug
Australia's Knowledge Gap on China

"Australia must develop the intellectual acumen to
see the world through China's leaders' eyes, in order
to manage the relationship on its own terms."

THE PROBLEM: If Australia wants to understand contemporary China as a foreign policy partner and a strategic actor, we need to proceed from a deeper understanding of the ruling Chinese Communist Party (CCP): its structures, its leaders and its military wing, the People's Liberation Army (PLA).

The CCP calls the shots in China, internally and externally. Unless we understand the Party's objectives, and how its leaders think and make decisions, our policies are likely to come up short. Australia's location, its alliance with the United States and its reliance upon China for trade mean that knowledge of the party leadership's machinations matters more to Australia than Cold War Kremlinology ever did.

The relationship with China is already complex, inter-weaving economic depth and political turbulence, including instances of CCP-directed interference in Australia's domestic affairs. The lengthening reach of the PLA into Australia's environs is bound to bring about more frequent strategic interaction and tension. The conduct of external policy in China is always subordinate to the Party's geopolitical direction and aims. Australia must develop the intellectual acumen to see the world through China's leaders' eyes, in order to manage the relationship on its own terms.

Foreign Minister Marise Payne recently announced a commitment of $44 million to "turbo-charge" Australia's relationship with China, via a new body, The National Foundation for Australia–China Relations. Its primary focus will apparently be to promote commercial diplomacy. Such a lopsided approach is unlikely to live up to the government's expectations without a corresponding investment into our understanding of how the CCP conducts China's business.

Unfortunately, China Studies, as a discipline, is not structured or incentivised to do this in Australia. Expertise on the CCP and PLA is dangerously thin across Australia's universities, and, to a lesser extent, think tanks. Since the mid-1990s, Australia has lost most of its empirical research expertise on China. Academia is not playing the role it should to raise Canberra's policy game and elevate the public debate. Universities are also incubators for Australia's next generation of China experts, who will populate government, business and academia itself.

Australia cannot afford to rely on external sources to supply the expertise needed to develop an informed set of policies towards China. Aspiring to greater self-reliance in defence capability and more "independent" diplomacy is fine in theory. But such aspirations will ring hollow without the concomitant ability to understand the outlook and motivations of China's ruling elites.

THE PROPOSAL: Australia needs to develop and retain more onshore academic expertise on the elite politics of the CCP and the PLA. The government should explicitly identify this as a knowledge gap for Australian universities to fill. Government and university leaders need to cooperate on long-term planning and investment to meet this requirement. Above all, we need to deconstruct the inner workings of the 89-million-strong CCP.

Critically, the focus of these efforts should be on investing in individuals rather than on setting up new centres. The underperformance of the Australian Centre on China in the World, set up in 2010 at the Australian National University and the recipient of $53 million in federal funding, is a salutary reminder of the potential wastage of the "centre-led" approach. An external review, completed last year, judged that the ANU's centre was "faltering and cannot be said to be meeting expectations".

Instead, resources should be invested in funded positions, scholarships and tied research programs to support and incentivise a new generation of China scholars specialising in CCP elite politics, the Party's influence over foreign policy, the PLA and other designated priority areas, such as cross-Strait relations. More doctoral research should be encouraged, provided there are enough qualified supervisors within academia. The government should be explicit in its riding instructions, but the conduct of research and academic appointments must be left to universities.

The resources should be spread to ensure a pool of expertise across universities and think tanks, to avoid overdependence on any one institution. Given the financial reliance of Australian universities upon China, including within the so-called Group of Eight, a diversified approach makes sense. This could be achieved by creating subject-specific networks that link universities and think tanks, and by selecting institutions that are less susceptible to self-censorship or pressure from pro-Beijing organisations, on or off campus. Unfortunately, academic freedom cannot be taken for granted on topics that are deemed sensitive by the CCP.

Extra government funding will help, but the primary problem is the willingness of government and universities to cooperate in allocating targeted resources. This touches raw nerves, as universities are rightfully protective of their intellectual independence, especially within the humanities. The initiative should extend beyond a generalised commitment to invest in China Studies. The study of Chinese culture, literature and philosophy is perfectly legitimate. Yet the chronic shortfall of China-literate expertise in the political and security fields is now such that it must be addressed head-on, and collaboratively.

WHY IT WILL WORK: Nurturing academic talent isn't overly costly; it is peanuts in proportion to the general tertiary education spend, and a drop in the ocean of defence procurement. Australia's political and military expertise on China can be turbo-charged for a fraction of the $44 million the government has recently committed to promoting Australia's exports to the PRC. Australia is already producing capable China scholars in these fields – the green shoots are there. But these individuals need career incentives, or they will go elsewhere.

This is a sensitive point, but universities should resist the temptation to hire PRC-trained academics as a quick fix to plug the expertise gap on elite politics. PRC-born Australians should of course be welcomed if they have received a liberal education outside of China. What Australia needs is a cohort of homegrown analysts, with the ability to read source material in Mandarin, who are motivated to pursue a career here, whether in academia or in government. Moreover, the China debate is too important to leave exclusively to country experts, some of whom have a vested interest in preserving their access and networks within the PRC. A healthy public discourse requires strategists, linguists, economists, historians and political scientists all to contribute, as each sees the "problem" from a different angle.

This proposal is intended not only as a fillip to better policy-making in Canberra. Academics should be informing the public debate and bridging an unhealthy gap in perception that has opened up on China, especially between those preoccupied with the Party's predatory and coercive statecraft, and those in business, with a more sanguine attitude towards the number-one trading partner.

Senior officials and diplomats could do more to engage leading scholars on China, including offering regular briefings and providing guidance from the intelligence community on partnership and interference risks. China experts schooled on elite politics and the PLA can contribute directly to government intelligence assessments by challenging or refining key judgements. There is already appetite for this within the Office of National Intelligence, which leads Australia's official assessments.

Concentrated investment and collaboration between government and academia is needed in order to build a cadre of China experts with the necessary language skills and knowledge to help Australia meet the complex policy challenges ahead. The payoff will be cumulative, not instantaneous. This is a long game – but a crucial one.

THE RESPONSE: The Minister for Education, Dan Tehan, said universities set their own curriculum and research direction and make decisions about hiring staff. He said the government was developing Australia's China knowledge and had funded the Australian Centre on China in the World at the Australian National University "to become a world leading institution for Chinese studies". "The Department of Foreign Affairs and Trade is investing in building the Australian government's capability and knowledge to advance Australia's foreign policy interests and priorities, including in countries such as China," he said in a statement.

Universities Australia, which represents thirty-nine universities, said Australian universities have significant expertise and research on China, including its politics, culture and history. It said the federal government was responsible for policy settings for research funding. "Greater public investment to enhance our understanding of our region and expand our national research capacity is always welcome. This is true of many fields with great strategic interest to our nation," it said in a statement. "Australia's research funding system is based on competitive grants awarded on recommendations from a process of expert peer review – as it should be – and the framework for this system is set by government." ■

Reviews

In Extremis: The Life of War Correspondent Marie Colvin
Lindsey Hilsum
Vintage

The Super Bowl professional football championship is the single biggest sporting event in America. The television audience is enormous – some 100 million people watched the game this year – allowing the network to charge corporations $10 million a minute to air their advertisements. These ads famously try to convince the captive audience, through wit or sentimentality, to buy the beer or the car, the food or the skin cream, for sale.

This year, one of those ads broke the mould. *The Washington Post* paid for a sober one-minute advertisement that wasn't selling anything. Instead, it extolled the virtue of a free press – in general, not just in relation to the iconic newspaper of the American capital.

That is how treacherous the mood has become in the United States. The president calls journalists "enemies of the people" and refers to any critical reporting as "fake news". Trump's vicious attacks are eroding confidence in the press, though its freedom is enshrined in the Constitution. And his remarks are cited by authoritarian leaders – such as Rodrigo Duterte of the Philippines and Hun Sen of Cambodia – who are attempting to solidify their power by eliminating an independent media.

So the *Washington Post* ad was a clear proclamation that the press refused to be bullied. Narrating over clips from World War II through to the civil rights marches and to the moon landing, actor Tom Hanks reminds the audience, "When we go to war, when we exercise our rights or when our nation is threatened, there is someone to gather the facts, to bring you the story no matter the cost."

At that moment, photographs of three journalists slowly pass across the screen. All three have been murdered for reporting the truth. Their very lives have been the "cost" of bringing their stories to the public.

One reporter has sleek golden hair and wears a black eye patch. She looked gamely into the camera with a half-smile, clearly a figure with pizzazz. She is Marie Colvin, the American war correspondent who was murdered by Syrian soldiers on orders from the government of Bashar al-Assad. In this image she was reporting from the besieged city of Homs, her pieces showing conclusively that government soldiers were systematically attacking civilians. By the Syrian government's calculation, Colvin had to be silenced. In killing her, Assad's army broke the international rules of war.

But Colvin is much more than a martyr. She is a striking symbol of the urgency and seriousness needed at this perilous moment to protect a society's right to an independent press. Colvin's articles dissected complicated problems and their consequences in places and circumstances where few other reporters ventured. Her life epitomised the unbearable hazards a correspondent often faces and the trauma and pain that spills over to their personal lives. Colvin's life and work are both worth remembering – not only for her contribution to journalism, but as a rebuttal to the toxic slurs uttered and illegal arrests made to quiet the free press.

In Extremis tells Colvin's fully lived story. This honest, often unsparing biography is written by Lindsey Hilsum, a friend and colleague, who reveals how such a complicated, courageous woman became one of the world's best war correspondents, and one of the most damaged.

Hilsum uses Colvin's diaries and letters to show how this Yale-educated American working for London's *Sunday Times* trained herself to accept the high cost of covering wars, to risk her life repeatedly and to absorb the emotional impact of all that senseless inhumanity in order to write articles that went beyond the stilted press releases and showed the damning truth.

Colvin grew to look the part. Her eye patch came after she lost an eye reporting on starvation in embattled Sri Lanka. Her elegance, even in the grotty precincts of combat, spoke to her refusal to be less than human even as the sacrifices of her profession upended her personal life. And her articles – above all, her articles – underline her singular, almost spiritual belief that her role was to write about the civilian victims of brutal wars. In her last interview, hours before she was murdered, she said that she had just witnessed a baby die.

Colvin came of age at a time when women had broken through many social barriers and were welcomed on foreign news staffs and assigned some of the roughest stories. The Middle East was her sweet spot. She went from Basra, Iraq, to Beirut, Lebanon, in her first month at *The Sunday Times*. She conducted exclusive interviews with Libyan leader Muamar al-Gathafi and Yasser Arafat of the Palestinian Liberation Organization.

Colvin established her own style of reportage, staying on the front lines longer than others, often ignoring the hardware of war to focus on the bloody consequences for civilians caught in crossfire and targeted attacks. This is from her article datelined *Beirut, 5 April 1987*: "She lay where she had fallen, face down on the dirt path leading out of Bourj el Baranjneh. Haji Achmed Ali, 22, crumpled as the snipers' bullets hit her in the face and stomach. She had tried to cross the no man's land between the Palestinian camp and the Amal militiamen besieging it to buy food for her family." Only a reporter risking the same fate could have written that powerful paragraph.

Colvin went on to the muddy killing fields of Bosnia. She made news herself in East Timor, where she refused to heed official warnings and stayed with refugees in a United Nations camp while Indonesian militia moved in to kill them. Her articles and interviews, along with those of two other women reporters who stayed, helped lift the siege.

Colvin was on a tear. She went next to the frozen frontlines of Chechnya, and then to Sri Lanka. The rebel Tamil Tigers had been fighting for over a decade to establish a separate homeland from the dominant Buddhist Sri Lankans. Colvin was promised an exclusive interview with the rebel leader and a first-hand account of the children starving because of boycotts in the war.

By now she was openly arguing with her editors when

they challenged the wisdom of her crossing into yet another risky rebel territory. She would have none of it. But in Sri Lanka the biggest story she wrote was how she lost her eye in crossfire. "Why do I cover wars?" she wrote afterwards. "I did not set out to be a war correspondent. It has always seemed to me that what I write about is humanity *in extremis*, pushed to the unendurable, and it is important to tell people what really happens in wars – declared and undeclared."

She railed against the routine praise for her as a *woman* war correspondent. Men were known simply as war correspondents. To her mind, being female should make no difference.

That may be true, but she was learning that as a woman she would suffer differently from her male colleagues. Underneath the boldness, she was cracking. Her private life was a near-shambles. Both her marriages failed as her husbands complained she was away too often and unable to be monogamous. Due to these separations, she lost the chance to have the children she thought she wanted. She was beginning to tally up the price of being a woman in her field.

Like many war correspondents,

Colvin suffered severe post-traumatic stress disorder after years of witnessing carnage on battlefields, of feeling fear and adrenaline mount as she waited for the next round of attacks. After losing her eye in Sri Lanka, she nearly became catatonic. She suffered waking nightmares. She was housebound, prone to shaking. She drank far too much and was endlessly questioning whether it was all worth it.

Fortunately, her employers recognised her distress and eventually convinced her to check into a clinic. Hilsum, a respected foreign correspondent herself, carefully dissects how Colvin resisted coddling but finally accepted treatment to lift her from profound depression and show her how to cope with those memories that would never disappear.

Several years later, Colvin addressed the general predicament of her tribe. "We always have to ask ourselves whether the level of risk is worth the story. What is bravery, and what is bravado?"

Colvin found her answer in an idealised version of Martha Gelhorn, the rare woman who succeeded as a World War II–era war correspondent – and came with more than a whiff of glamour, as a former wife of Ernest Hemingway.

At first glance, Gelhorn is an odd choice as a role model. She was working in a time when women weren't allowed near most battlefields. Women didn't become combat reporters in numbers until the Vietnam War. But Gelhorn made her reputation covering what she called the face of war, the brutal images that "are the strongest argument against war". Gelhorn was a fellow spirit from another era – who also watched her personal life fall apart in the pursuit of a "crusade on behalf of those without a voice in society".

When Syrian intelligence finally pinpointed Colvin's hiding place in Homs in 2012 and targeted her and her colleagues, she had negotiated some of her challenges and was determined to carry on her work.

Wa'el al-Omar, her guide in Homs, was one of the last people to see her alive. "I knew her for a short period, but it was a time of life or death," he said. "She dreamed of being a voice for the weak, and of a place where war doesn't affect civilians. She wasn't childish or naïve, but she was idealistic. She was a dreamer."

What better moment than now to appreciate everything required to write those articles from war, to translate those intense moments of humanity *in extremis*? This remarkable and sensitive biography is a rebuttal to every bully or coward who accuses a journalist like Colvin of being an "enemy of the people", to every frightened politician who denounces independent journalism as "fake news".

Last year alone, sixty-three journalists were killed doing their jobs around the world; half of them were deliberately targeted, according to Reporters Without Borders. For the first time, the United States was listed as one of the five most dangerous countries to be a journalist, joining India and Mexico, where reporters were also killed in rampages. A.G. Sulzberger, the publisher of *The New York Times*, asked Trump in person this year to stop his anti-press ravings. The effects, he said "are being felt all over the world, including [by] folks who are literally putting their lives on the line to report the truth".

The president made no such commitment.

This year, an American court found the Syrian government guilty of murdering Colvin by targeted shelling – a reminder that the messenger relaying these truths often suffers as much as the soldier fighting the wars.

Elizabeth Becker

Common Enemies: Crime, Policy and Politics in Australia– Indonesia Relations
Michael McKenzie
Oxford University Press

The Mexicans have a saying that perfectly illustrates the nature of their neighbourhood: *So far from God, so close to the United States.* Closer to home, there is a whole body of literature about two other odd neighbours, Indonesia and Australia. In recent decades, a common thesis is that this couple represents a "relationship in recurrent crisis" – a claim based on controversies over issues such as beef, boats, spying and treatment of drug mules and Indonesian fishermen.

But crisis was not the dominant feeling during my five years (from 2005 to 2010) as ambassador in Jakarta. The two countries had fallings-out during those years over the granting of asylum to Papuan Indonesians, New South Wales' disgraceful treatment of the Jakarta governor during an official visit, and various issues relating to people smuggling. There were certainly moments of bad blood and bruised feelings. On the other hand, there were interactions that generated quite different responses, notably the Australian assistance following the Aceh tsunami in December 2004. It was also a period of joint work in a range of areas, including agriculture, health, regional initiatives and education in eastern Indonesia – the sorts of things that do not often attract headlines.

In *Common Enemies,* Michael McKenzie deals with developments in the handling of major law-enforcement issues between the two countries since the 1970s. He writes with first-hand experience, both as an officer in the attorney-general's department in Canberra and as legal counsellor in the Australian embassy in Jakarta.

McKenzie sets out to analyse the extensive cooperation on criminal justice between the two countries, and to make suggestions about strategies for future cooperation. The result is engrossing. He supports his argument with reference to more than one hundred interviews he conducted with Australians and Indonesians involved in areas such as counterterrorism, extradition and people smuggling. The interviews show that what was a modest level of bilateral police cooperation prior to the 2002 Bali bombings has become a relationship of mutual trust and respect. When in Jakarta, I observed the way this relationship worked in the counterterrorism sphere, where the AFP provided intelligence to the Indonesian national police, who acted on it,

and rightly gained public acclaim for their successful operations.

The book is at its best in illustrating the ways in which Indonesian and Australian police personnel have interacted with one another over the past twenty years. The interviews evoke the sense of collegiality that has been fostered both by the common objective of preventing crime and by a shared language of law enforcement.

McKenzie argues convincingly that an essential element in the Australia–Indonesia relationship is a perception that the cooperation benefits both countries. This has persisted through periods of tension, such as the acrimony that followed the 2013 allegations of Australian bugging operations targeting Indonesian president Susilo Bambang Yudhoyono, his wife and senior officials. The value of the relationship has only been questioned when that sense of mutual benefit becomes strained. McKenzie gives as an example a period when Indonesia believed that Australia was not sufficiently expediting extradition requests, despite explanations from Australia about the delays inherent in its legal system. This thesis rings true to me, and reminds me of the way the AFP, proven deliverers for Indonesia in the counterterrorism sphere, secured a high level of engagement from the Indonesian police in anti-people-smuggling work, which was not an Indonesian priority.

To McKenzie, the bilateral relationship has two core dimensions: governmental, involving pursuing political interests, and bureaucratic, involving officials and organisations pursuing policy interests. He argues that there is a tension between these political and policy interests, which results from the differences between the various key players, including private actors such as the media. But he draws perhaps too sharp a line between the interests and actions of what he terms the political and the policy players. His argument is, essentially, that "national politicians are forever playing to their domestic constituencies" and "political parochialism and policy ambition pull against each other".

McKenzie is undoubtedly correct that from time to time political differences have dogged the pursuit of enduring interests. A scorecard might well include difficulties caused by Indonesia, particularly in its pre-democratic phase, such as hostilities over the birth of Malaysia in the 1960s and the occupation of East Timor from the 1970s, as well as sensitivities over the independence of East Timor in the late 1990s and early 2000s. It would record instances of mutual misunderstanding, for example over the granting of refugee visas to Papuan asylum seekers in 2006. More pointedly, it would also record instances of thoughtlessness, provocation, single-minded pursuit of domestic political agendas and, occasionally, stupidity. Witness Australia's decision in 2011 to ban live cattle exports to Indonesia; both governments' ratcheting-up of rhetoric and action over the members of the Bali Nine between 2005 and 2015; the 2018 embassy in Israel affair; and of course boats.

But there would also be high moments, such as our ready assistance to Indonesia after the Aceh tsunami and the economic crises of 1998 and 2008, as well as concerted efforts by Australian governments of all persuasions to promote a substantial relationship with Indonesia. These efforts include the Lombok Treaty on security cooperation, the Comprehensive Strategic Partnership Agreement, the New Colombo Plan and the Closer Economic Partnership Agreement. Further remarkable action at the political level has been joint Australian–Indonesian promotion of regional initiatives over the past twenty years in areas such as counterterrorism, sustainable fisheries and disaster preparedness.

Overall, McKenzie provides good evidence for the argument that law-enforcement agencies have, generally, been able to pursue activities of mutual benefit. And in my experience the same is true of working relationships in other areas, as diverse as transport safety and security, immigration processing, government financial services, the functioning of courts and audit offices, and defence and development cooperation.

All this matters because, if anything, Indonesia's transition to democracy has increased the chances of short-term political differences between the two countries. There was no biting of fingernails on election eve in Jakarta during the thirty-plus years of the autocratic New Order, and the essential bilateral dynamic involved Australia working things out with the Indonesian president. If we had him on board, other institutions generally fell into line; and, on important issues such as APEC, the understandings with Suharto were crucial to Australian aims.

Today, governments in both countries face constant media scrutiny, assertive parliaments and civil society, opinion polls and all the other messiness of democracy. This does sometimes lead to our two countries yelling past each other, but there is also a mutual recognition in our better moments that some things are intended for a domestic audience. And, I would argue, the trials that result from our shared democratic processes are a price we should be prepared to pay. Just as we should – despite the setbacks or crises – continue to work together across a range of mutually beneficial areas.

Bill Farmer

Army of None:
Autonomous Weapons
and the Future of War
Paul Scharre
WW Norton & Company

nventive humans have created
many good technological servants,
some of which turn out to be bad
masters. "Unmanned aerial
systems", or commercial drones,
can help locate lost hikers, fugitives
and bushfires, although we have to
keep them away from airports.
Artificial intelligence can enable
facial recognition of our passport
photos and sharing of biomedical
data (as long as it is efficiently
managed). Swarms of armed robots
can search and destroy enemy
targets. At the outer extreme are AI
devices with "deep learning" that can
spontaneously change their "mind"
and attack of their own volition.
Some don't "know" when to stop.

But when AI is not well
managed, the communications of
Parliament House, including elector
lists and the personal details of
politicians, can be hacked. Worse
occurs when AI becomes the master,
not the servant, as two recent Boeing
737 Max 8 crashes showed.

Regulation of the multi-billion-
dollar AI industry is racing to catch
up with invention. In the space of a
decade, thirty nations have acquired
cyberwarfare capacity, using it for
sophisticated espionage as well as
offensive sabotage of financial
systems, infrastructure and
communications. Terrorists of the
future will create destruction and
seize publicity not by hijacking aircraft
but by crashing drones into them and
hacking aviation systems. David E.
Sanger, chief Washington
correspondent for *The New York
Times* and author of *The Perfect
Weapon*, notes that the leading nations
in cyber conflict are the United States,
the United Kingdom, Israel, Iran,
China, Russia and North Korea, and
that computer code has become the
"ultimate leveller among nations".

Stephen Hawking, Elon Musk
and Apple co-founder Steve Wozniak
have predicted a global AI arms race.

President Putin claims that whichever nation or group leads in AI will rule the world, and China is investing in becoming the dominant AI power by 2030. Having pioneered AI, the United States now lags behind in its development, which is why Trump earlier this year signed an executive order on "Maintaining American Leadership in AI".

Paul Scharre's book, with its nerdy appearance and enigmatic title, doesn't promise a fascinating read, although in small print on the cover there's praise from Bill Gates. A former US Army Ranger in Iraq and Afghanistan, Scharre knows his stuff, and interviews knowledgeable people in the fields of defence, intelligence, law and human rights, explaining in layperson's language the workings of killer robots and autonomous weapons, before considering the alarming risks of error, malfunction and failure.

The text includes a chart showing humanity's efforts to ban various weapons, starting with poisoned or barbed arrows in 1500 BC and moving through various firearms, aerial warfare, chemical and bacteriological weapons, to nuclear and cluster bombs, satellites and space weapons. It's a chilling summary of humans' inventiveness in killing and maiming one another. Scharre discusses the numerous near-misses with autonomous weapons, for which either human error or the technology was to blame. An informant confesses to him that she is more afraid of autonomous weapons than of nuclear bombs – not because they are more destructive but because once created, they will more certainly be used.

Starting with a chapter called "Robocalypse Now", Scharre recognises the influence of fantasy and science-fiction films, such as *Flight of the Navigator*, *Ex Machina* and the documentary *Eye in the Sky*. Scientists and defence experts take these seriously and discuss them, and champions of chess and the Japanese strategy game Go have had interesting encounters with AI. The robots of Isaac Asimov's books, governed by his three laws, cannot harm humans (and a fourth law, proposed by James Bridie, requires that they be able to explain themselves to humans). The droids in *Star Wars* are our willing servants. But in the *Matrix* series, robots enslave humans, and in *Terminator*, Skynet identifies humans as a threat to its existence and mounts an extermination attack. Reagan's real-life Star Wars missile shield was intended to alarm the USSR by creating the impression the United States could survive a nuclear first strike, while the joint chiefs of staff reportedly knew it would not work or even be built, but wanted the huge funding it would deliver. Could cyberwar deterrence be similarly ineffective and expensive, and have the same objective?

Scharre concludes that AI is with us to stay, but "collectively, humanity has choices" about what to do with it. The world's nations and individuals can and will use AI for good and bad purposes, but they must make a "conscious choice to pull back from weapons that are too dangerous, too inhumane". His "must" is not reassuring: in the end, after giving due weight to diverse opinions about that choice, all he can advise is restraint.

Regulation and international law are not adequately nuanced to deal with AI, Scharre finds, although rules about specific robots, and nations' behaviour in cyberspace, are being negotiated. Since 2016 an expert group under the UN Convention on Certain Conventional Weapons has been discussing autonomous weapons, but still has produced no workable definition, let alone a multinational treaty to ban them. In a world where everything can become a weapon, Scharre observes, military powers are not interested in a treaty. Progress will require establishing specific categories of weapons and creating restrictions on them one at a time, and – more problematically – on their users.

Scharre's patriotism occasionally overrides his objectivity. The US has since 2002 conducted targeted killings using drones, which he doesn't mention. He says that China "is building a techno-dystopian surveillance state" aimed at controlling all its citizens. But this, minus the adjective, is just what Edward Snowden revealed the United States was doing. Russians anticipate a robotised unit that can conduct military operations independently: the same capacity preoccupies the United States. An American professor of law declares that weapons bans and international humanitarian law (IHL) mean nothing to "odious regimes" in Iraq, Libya and Syria, which "would never respect IHL in the first place". Yet Scharre does not mention that the United States rejects the International Court of Justice, the International Criminal Court and the application of IHL to itself, nor that the United States and Israel in 2010 used the Stuxnet virus to disable Iran's nuclear facility. The threat of militarised AI is serious, including from our ally. Americans would be wise to lead by example, before other states or individuals use cyberweapons on them.

Alison Broinowski

Myanmar's "Rohingya" Conflict
Anthony Ware and
Costas Laoutides
Hurst Publishers

This time of year, over the verdant paddies, deforested hills and tea-brown waterways of Rakhine State, every molecule of air seems to swell to bursting, and it's a relief when the pressure plummets and the dark skies unleash their torrents.

The rains serve as something of an enforced half-time in the conflict between the insurgent group the Arakan Army and Myanmar's armed forces, the Tatmadaw: at some point, the monsoons make it untenable to maintain full-scale hostilities, and the number of clashes dips. It is especially needed this year. In Rakhine State, the first half of 2019 has seen a severe escalation in fighting. The clashes have displaced tens of thousands, and left scores dead.

The Arakan Army is battling for autonomy from the Central Burmese state, which it views as an illegitimate colonising presence. In 2016 and 2017, Rakhine State was the site of a genocidal purge of the Rohingya, a Muslim people who were formerly the majority in the far north-west. In this new Arakan Army–Tatmadaw conflict, both Muslims and Buddhists are contributing to the body count. Civilians have been caught in the crossfire – and landmines don't discriminate.

Across the border in Bangladesh, in the shanty slums of the world's largest refugee camp, people subsist in a tarpaulin city that is becoming increasingly permanent. For the almost one million Rohingya refugees in Bangladesh, the arrival of the rains heralds fresh concerns about the management of human waste, hillside collapses, contamination from shallow graves, the threat of disease and the possibility of cyclone. People want to go home, but "home" as they know it is gone. In the absence of meaningful action to reserve property rights for the exiled, the scorched earth where villages and farms used to be risks being swept up in one of the more impressive land grabs in Myanmar's history – by a state that excels at them.

In the year or so after the biblical-scale exodus tapered off, Myanmar and Bangladesh accused each other of stalling on a deal to repatriate the refugees. As this new Arakan Army–Tatmadaw conflict worsens, talk of allowing returns has all but disappeared. The government's ability to administer the western state has been severely curtailed amid mass resignations of village leaders and several assassinations. The floodlit, barbed-wire-enclosed accommodation blocks that Myanmar built to process returnees remain unused.

In Rakhine, hundreds of thousands of Rohingya Muslims remain interned in camps and villages, subject to movement restrictions under a policy that no one seems to be able to produce in document form. This has led to aid dependence, and Muslim communities struggle to access livelihoods, education and healthcare. As the Tatmadaw seeks to flush out Arakan Army insurgents, there have been reports of forced labour and mass detention – and, in one instance, the summary execution of six men.

Anecdotally, the Tatmadaw's violence in Rakhine may have given rise to something many believed impossible: empathy between the Buddhist and Muslim civilian communities of the divided state. Perhaps not surprisingly, there's a joke among expat non-government organisation workers in Myanmar: when discussing Rakhine, the expression "it's complex" is the trump card.

Until fairly recently, there were few books on Rakhine State. In the past three years there has been Francis Wade's *Myanmar's Enemy Within* and Azeem Ibrahim's *The Rohingyas* – and now there is *The "Rohingya" Conflict*, by Australian academics "Anthony Ware" and "Costas Laoutides" (the latter two sets of quotation marks mine, although that, apparently, is their preferred form of identification).

The pair are at pains to strike a middle path, and offer a detached, impartial overview of the beleaguered state, examining the conflict from a range of angles. They did conduct extensive fieldwork, but the reader could be forgiven for not realising this from the text, leaving aside a brief reference in the preface. (I only know the extent of their work because I met Ware in the city of Sittwe.) It's to the detriment of the reader's understanding of aspects such as movement restrictions that the reality on the ground isn't demonstrated with working examples. The determination to keep the focus high-level too often renders the book devoid of colour and lacking in resonance. Often, the discussion of systematic human-rights abuses is swathed in the euphemistic language of development-speak.

In Myanmar, locals voice frustration with what they see as a reductive and one-sided narrative pushed by the Western media, which they say favours stories of Rohingya victimhood and rejoices in criticising Aung San Suu Kyi. The idea of a conspiracy to push a unified line suggests they've never had to organise anything involving journalists, or dealt with the United Nations. Any bias in coverage is far more likely due to the Myanmar government making it damn near impossible to report freely from inside the state. Reuters staff, including former colleagues of mine, have been jailed for reporting the facts of conflict. So it is unfortunate, also, that the authors do not offer on-the-ground examples because in recent times, travel permits have become infinitely harder to come by.

It is clear the authors intend *The "Rohingya" Conflict* to serve as an aid to constructive engagement and perhaps even influence. It presents a synthesis of other sources, and could serve as a companion guide for the newly arrived diplomat or aid worker who wants to be able to understand the context, including the intractable argument over which group emerged on which side of a border that didn't then exist, but who lacks the diligence to read the *New Mandala* comments section, or to comb through human-rights reports from the 1990s.

In the business capital of Yangon, translators and bootleggers tend to make quick work of reproducing texts on Myanmar, then flogging them on the street to passers-by, though the accuracy of the texts cannot be guaranteed. It's unfortunate that, as far as information online tells me, there is no official Burmese translation being released. The usefulness of a book like this to ground actors is limited.

I often wonder if government and UN officials working at a policy level have any clue exactly how grim things are on the ground, and I puzzle at how even the façade of a discussion on repatriation can be maintained when it is evident that those exiled will not be returning home soon: it will not be safe for the foreseeable future. Key to understanding the gap between policy and reality are the stories of individuals in the towns, villages and internment camps of Rahkine State – something the government's media clampdown has tried to silence.

Myanmar is slated to head to the ballot box in 2020. Fighting will likely die down somewhat in the months to come, as nature dictates a time-out. It remains to be seen whether free and fair elections can and will take place; if conflict continues to escalate, it is possible that a state of emergency could be declared in parts of Rakhine. For both the ruling National League for Democracy and the unpopular military-backed Union Solidarity and Development Party, this would not be a tragedy – the Rakhine ethnic bloc continues to consolidate. As they say, it's complex.

Kayleigh Long

The Great Successor:
The Secret Rise and
Rule of Kim Jong Un
Anna Fifield
John Murray

Writing and commentary on North Korea are routinely crippled by our poor knowledge of its inner workings. The government publishes few formal documents or White Papers for outsiders, provides little hard data such as calculations of annual economic growth or national budget figures, and routinely exaggerates or lies in its propaganda. So we often rely on logic or parallels to now-defunct Stalinist states to make estimations of its motivations. In her biography of North Korean Supreme Leader Kim Jong-un, Anna Fifield has tried hard to push beyond these limitations, chasing leads around the world and reaching out directly to dozens if not hundreds of interviewees, including many North Korean defectors. This gives the book a powerful credibility.

Fifield, now *The Washington Post*'s correspondent in Beijing but who previously covered Japan and the Koreas, has a journalist knack for colour and detail, which brings her narrative alive. Her lengthy treatment of the pampered yet lonely life of North Korean elites is an excellent example. North Korea has been ruled by three generations of the Kim family. The various children, retainers, mistresses and hangers-on in that cloistered world live in unbelievable opulence. Fearing assassination or other harm, and to ensure that regular North Koreans have little sense of their Neronian lifestyle, these elites are not allowed to mingle much with the public. Consequently, they are strikingly lonely in their palaces, which might account for their otherwise curious efforts to attend an Eric Clapton concert or slip into Disneyland Japan.

Early on, Fifield covers the emergence of the Kim dynasty and the various competitors to Kim

Jong-un. The most famous of these is Kim Jong-nam, whom Kim Jong-un had murdered with VX toxin in Kuala Lumpur International Airport in 2017. Fifield's coverage of the current dictator's early years is arguably her most important contribution. While the politics of Kim's reign likely interests readers more, it is also widely covered elsewhere. Conversely, his early life is poorly known, and this is certainly the thickest, best-researched treatment of it I have seen. Fifield shows her investigative chops by jetting off to Switzerland, where Kim went to school, and poking around among those who knew him. She learned that Kim was far more interested in basketball than study, struggled to connect with other students and skipped class routinely for family reasons. This only partial immersion in the Westernised environment of Switzerland may explain why his schooling there did not much nurture liberalising or reformist impulses.

The heart of the book is the consolidation of power by this newest Kim monarch. Kim was just twenty-seven when he became the Supreme Leader of the North. Many thought he would become a figurehead of the army or his deceased father's retainers. There was much scepticism that such a young, untested man – Kim had never served in either the party or the army, North Korea's two core institutions – would triumph in North Korea's Confucian-gerontocratic elite system. Yet he did.

Fifield makes clear that Kim is now fully in charge. She charts how he sidelined competitors, brought the army under control, and used money and luxury to co-opt the elites. She references Machiavelli's *The Prince* in describing this consolidation, and that seems apt. Particularly gripping is her rise-and-fall narrative of Kim's uncle, Jang Song-thaek. After becoming a central figure behind the throne of Kim's father, he was harshly purged in the son's new order. It is an archetypal story of the dangerous politics of closed autocratic systems, and Fifield tells it with brio.

The most policy-relevant portion of the book is its final chapters, which focus on the regime's nuclear and missile development, and subsequent efforts to strike a deal with South Korea and the United States. Fifield is guardedly optimistic. She believes – correctly, to my mind – that Kim is genuinely looking for a deal and that he might trade some of his nukes and missiles for international acceptance, but certainly not all of them. She notes, and again I agree, that Kim came to power determined to complete the nuclear and missile programs his father and grandfather had haltingly pursued. Unlike them, Kim launched a determined, years-long series of tests, culminating in 2017 with the detonation of a fusion warhead – whose yield is an order of magnitude greater than the atomic weapons the United States used in World War II – and the launch of an intercontinental ballistic missile that could strike the US eastern seaboard.

With these successes, North Korea achieved a decades-old goal. It could now threaten the United States with massive nuclear retaliation. Mutually assured destruction with America all but guaranteed that the United States would never attack North Korea, or otherwise pursue regime change, due to the threat that Pyongyang would, in turn, launch a nuclear weapon at the US homeland. Regime security for the Kim family had at last been achieved.

Nuclear deterrence in hand,

Kim could then turn to relieving the sanctions and containment his country faced. Since 2018, Kim has downplayed his nuclear weapons and missiles and talked up diplomacy and outreach. Most importantly, he met US President Donald Trump twice in an effort to broker a deal relieving the North's isolation. Trump seems to believe that his fulsome personality and negotiating skills brought Kim to the bargaining table. Fifield avoids directly refuting this interpretation, but she does repeatedly note how staged and choreographed Kim's coming out feels. At one point, she aptly terms it a "contrived metamorphosis". The correlate of that, then, is that North Korea's turn towards diplomacy had nothing to do with Trump's "friendship" or bargaining skills but was in fact a long-planned manoeuvre after completing the nuclear deterrent. That is almost certainly accurate.

Given the interest in North Korea's Supreme Leader in recent years, and the curious dearth of biographical treatments, Fifield's book will be read widely. It covers a lot of territory, and some of it – on Kim's youthful years – breaks new ground. Fifield makes sure to sprinkle throughout her story the grandiloquent language the North Korean media uses to describe Kim. This adds a bit of levity to an otherwise grim account. Kim has such wonderful titles as "Invincible and Triumphant General", "Sun of Socialism" and "Ever-Victorious, Iron-Willed Commander".

If there is any downside to the book, it is that the chronological framing leads to topical disjunctures as we leap from nuclear weapons to Dennis Rodman (whom Kim wanted to meet personally several years ago) to Kim family decadence, and so on. But this is limited by the author's wise decision to avoid the ridiculous gossip that surrounds the Kim family. For example, the notion that the Kims are mad is quickly and appropriately dismissed. Rodman gets the necessary coverage but no more.

Fifield's tone is serious and the coverage rich. Recommended.

Robert E. Kelly

Correspondence

"Red Detachment"
by Linda Jaivin

Clive Hamilton

In her essay "Red Detachment" (AFA5: *Are We Asian Yet?*), Linda Jaivin includes a patronising commentary on my book *Silent Invasion: China's Influence in Australia.* Headed "We need to talk about Clive", the commentary betrays a conceit behind the practice of Australian Sinology: that Australia's China experts are the only ones entitled to talk about China, and their other favourite subject, themselves.

The Sinological conceit goes something like this. To speak authoritatively about China, you need years of immersion in its language, culture and history. Once you have mastered these disciplines, you are authorised to talk about yourself as a noted Sinologist. Jaivin explains that as a noted Sinologist she and the in-group of fellow experts have a privileged role explaining China to the rest of us.

The rest of us would probably accept this conceit if the Sinological community had done its job alerting Australians to the risks to national sovereignty and the integrity of our democratic institutions associated with this country's unfettered engagement with China in recent years. It did next to nothing.

Australia's Sinologists were certainly not starved of resources. With the help of a $53 million endowment from Kevin Rudd pumped into a Sinology centre at the Australian National University, they could have run a whole program on China's influence and interference operations in Australia, and the risks to Chinese-Australian communities of being co-opted into the Chinese Communist Party's "great rejuvenation of the Chinese people". Instead, they frittered the resources away developing their "nuanced" approach to China and Chinese culture.

Jaivin sets herself up as willing to tackle the awkward subject of "Clive" but goes on to discuss herself. Clive, you see, does not speak Chinese and so makes mistakes, like not reporting the complicated political history of a popular song to which he refers. If only he had read my book, then he would understand. If he had asked me about the cultural meaning and depth of the song, he would not "quake" over "Chinese culture" but be "astonished" by it.

At the 2008 Olympic torch relay, Jaivin may well have felt astonishment at the spectacle of thousands of angry, red-draped Chinese students outside Canberra's Parliament House, chanting CCP slogans and singing patriotic songs while screaming at and hitting Tibetan protesters. I quaked. Perhaps I would have relaxed if I had understood the cultural history of the words they were shouting. I'm not sure about the Tibetans.

Jaivin attributes the cold turn in the bilateral relationship that has taken place over the last two years to an upsurge in Sinophobia. Our "quaking and shaking" over China has "reached fever pitch", she writes. Really? Had she read my book's 100,000 words of analysis, supported by scores of examples and 1200 footnotes (all checked in draft by four Chinese-fluent experts), she would have found that the icy turn in the relationship is not a "China-panic" but reflects Australians like me simply waking up to the fact that for many years the CCP has been engaged in a systematic campaign of influence and subversion in this country.

The fact that she has not yet woken up to this does not mean that the rest of us are panicking. We are just making up for lost time doing what she and her colleagues should have done years ago.

In addition to coercing some elements of the Chinese diaspora to work for the Party, the campaign has been aimed at winning over Australia's elites, including our intellectual elites. In *Silent Invasion*, I discuss a wide range of people in business, politics, the media, universities, community groups and cultural organisations who – for reasons including sheer naivety, financial incentive, political gain and actual commitment to the CCP – act in ways that enhance the Party's influence in Australia, undermining national security and sovereignty. For Jaivin, these are no more than "people who believe in continued engagement with China", and she includes herself among them.

As scales fall from Australian eyes, it's especially galling when these elites tell us there is nothing to be seen here, that it's just anti-Chinese racism and

"Cold War thinking" – and, in the case of our Sinologists, that we need to adopt a "nuanced" approach to China. The same handfuls of sand are thrown in our eyes by the Department of Propaganda in Beijing.

While all academics are prone to professional jealousy, it's never a good look to express it publicly. Jaivin is not the first to say, "I know more than Clive Hamilton; I should have written a book on this topic." To which I say, "Yes, you should have. But you didn't." In fact, being a Sinologist is not a qualification for writing a book like *Silent Invasion* because it's less about China than it is about Australian politics and society. On that score, I am probably better qualified to speak on the Chinese Communist Party's influence in Australia than the august group of China scholars who wrote an open letter attempting to shut down debate, declaring that they "could see no evidence" of interference, a declaration that looks more foolish by the month.

All the same, in writing *Silent Invasion* I benefited enormously from the intellectual generosity of several China experts here and abroad, including in China. If my book is another outburst of Australian Sinophobia, it's a reading that must have been missed by the Chinese and Chinese-Australians who supported me in the research process and by the large number of Chinese-Australians who gathered in Sydney in March 2018 to launch the book.

The anti-Chinese racism that Jaivin can read between the lines in *Silent Invasion* must have also escaped the scrutiny of the publishers of the recent Chinese-language edition in Taiwan. Or perhaps they could all see what she could not: that the book is not about Chinese people at all, but about the CCP. Of course, Jaivin will complain that she knows the difference between the people and the Party, yet her writing shows that she repeatedly blurs the two. That is the deep problem with so much China scholarship in this country.

Clive Hamilton, professor of public ethics at Charles Sturt University and author of Silent Invasion: China's Influence in Australia

Barry Li

always thought I knew a lot about China, until I started writing my first book about it. Before I read Linda Jaivin's article, I thought I knew about *The Red Detachment of Women* too. It is a classic. Almost every person from mainland China can immediately recall the signature lyrics from the film: *In ancient China, Mulan [yes, the same Mulan known to the rest of the world through the Disney cartoon] went to join the army for her father; today, the women's army hold their guns for the people . . .*

For some reason, I always thought the Women's Army in *The Red Detachment* fought against Japanese invaders. I bet if you asked ten Chinese people under the age of forty, "Who did the Women's Army fight against?" you would receive ten different answers. Most of the younger generation, who must have watched every episode of *Doraemon*, would not know all the names of the eight model operas of the Cultural Revolution. These shows were the classics of the last century. The younger generation spend their money on K-pop concerts or local productions of Broadway musicals. For this reason, I found the labelling of *The Red Detachment* as "political propaganda" amusing rather than concerning.

To me, the issue is not whether *The Red Detachment* is political propaganda – it clearly is. The issue is that some people in Australia, mostly former residents of China who object to communism and have bad memories of living under it, may feel uncomfortable when this clearly "communist art" is performed in a country such as Australia, which has traditionally been seen as removed from the threat of any "communist influence". The demonstrators presumably believed that this performance was organised using "communist money" by the country from which they had escaped. While I think no amount of foreign money used for artistic works or cultural influence can damage the values and beliefs of the Australian people, the misunderstanding and conflict of opinions among the Chinese communities in Australia are a real concern.

I'm glad that Jaivin also mentioned the 2009 documentary *The 10 Conditions of Love* and Uyghur rights in China. Let's put aside, if we can, what the government is doing in Xinjiang for now. The issue raises questions about relations between the "majority" and "minorities", similar to questions we have in Australia. Take me, for example – as a typical Han Chinese, I always considered Xinjiang to be Chinese territory. I also always considered everyone living in Xinjiang to be Chinese, just like me. I believed (according to the Chinese constitution) that the Uyghur people had all the rights that Han Chinese have. But how much do I really know about these people? How much do I know about their language, culture, art and opinions? Do most Han Chinese even care? I bet not.

My knowledge about the Uyghur culture is very superficial – it is limited to their food, music and dancing. As a child, one of my favourite cartoon characters was Afanti, from a Chinese clay-animation program – a legendary wise Uyghur man who always tricked and defeated the evil and greedy Uyghur landlord Bayi. Was it "communist propaganda"? Maybe. The storylines of most "communist art" are quite simple. They are not so different from cartoons for children, just crueller. In these types of programs, things are always black and white. Choices are clear-cut, never controversial, and no one is complicated. There are always pure "heroes" and totally unforgivable "evildoers" who have to be physically eliminated. There's no room for negotiation, let alone co-existence.

When it comes to the Uyghurs, the Han Chinese people, as the dominant majority, are self-centred (including in the way they help and embrace minorities). I didn't realise this until I came to Australia and became a member of a minority myself. I think I'm safe to say that the majority of white Aussies know very little about Chinese history and culture.

For those Han Chinese in China who try to understand and respect minorities, there is a knowledge gap, just as there is for many Australians in this country. I know that most "good" Aussies are doing their best to understand and respect my origins and culture. The effort is visible.

And among these "good" Australians, there's Jaivin. In this essay about *The Red Detachment* she astonished me with her extensive knowledge and deep understanding of contemporary Chinese art and culture, as well as the complicated political issues involved. If I have to point out a weakness of the essay, it is this: while the issues have been identified and discussed in depth – and there is clearly a need for Australians to better understand Chinese culture and politics – I don't see any clear recommendations or solutions.

But the difficulty in offering such solutions is obvious. After all, no one has any feasible plan. Only time can solve complicated issues like these.

And it's much easier talking than doing. There is much criticism of those who are actually doing the work to bridge the cultural gaps. For this reason, I respect the organisers of *The Red Detachment* in Australia, who stuck to their guns under significant pressure. I also appreciate those with different political views who stood up and demonstrated in public. I suppose this is the point of a free society, in which different voices and demands can be heard, and different opinions and interpretations of art can be appreciated. People can agree to disagree – then, through friction and balancing, we reach an acceptable common ground. This to me, is how the "art of democracy" fundamentally differs from the "art of communism".

Barry Li, author of The New Chinese: How They Are Shaping Australia

Linda Jaivin responds

The risible notion that I have ever referred to myself as a "noted Sinologist" is just one of the many fanciful accusations that Clive Hamilton flings my way in his response to my essay. Another is that I belong to some kind of cabal of China academics who are allegedly averse to criticising the Chinese state or its influence in Australia because we have invested so much time studying the Chinese language and Chinese history. Hamilton attributes fabricated quotations to me using inverted commas, including one in which I wish I had written a book on China's influence in Australia (I don't, actually), and attacks me for what I never said. Falsely attributed quotations and the invention of conspiracies are, coincidentally, tactics also favoured by the Chinese Communist Party. For the record, I'm a freelance writer, editor and translator, not a salaried academic.

To accuse me of being blind to Chinese operations in Australia is simply more evidence-free bizarreness on Hamilton's part. To suggest that I would happily rationalise, on any grounds, Chinese students' aggression towards pro-Tibetan protesters at the April 2008 Olympic torch relay in Canberra borders on defamatory. I wrote and spoke about the torch relay in various forums, including in an essay published in *The Monthly* in August that year. That piece also discussed death threats to a journalist friend from soi-disant Chinese nationalists for her reporting on human rights abuses in Tibet. The fact that I don't agree in every detail with Hamilton's arguments doesn't make me an amoral idiot.

My essay addresses the practical and ethical challenges of engaging with Chinese culture, as well as the rewards of doing so. It in no way sidesteps the reality of China's one-party dictatorship. It also acknowledges the work Hamilton has done in bringing Beijing's operations in Australia to public attention.

I've given flak to some of the same people he targets, and on similar grounds. But I maintain that his more extreme claims – that Beijing wants to turn Australia into a tribute state, for instance – are overblown; just like, apparently, his antipathy to criticism. It appears that if you don't jump straight onto his bandwagon, and pitch your tent there, you're classed a panda hugger, appeaser or member of the "China lobby".

Hamilton regrets that the scholars of the Australian Centre on China in the World (CIW) at the Australian National University "could have run a whole program on China's influence and interference operations in Australia" but instead "frittered the resources away developing their 'nuanced' approach to China and Chinese culture". Leaving aside the odd suggestion that an academic institution should devote itself to banging a single drum, on which there are already plenty of sticks, including that of Hamilton himself, it seems self-evident that there is great value in cultivating a "nuanced" approach to China and Chinese culture. The CIW also works on Chinese economics, politics, demographics, foreign affairs and other topics, drawing on all disciplines in an approach its founder, Geremie Barmé, called "New Sinology", which is based on familiarity with the Chinese language, culture and history. I am not sure which dictionary Hamilton is using, but in mine, "nuanced" is not a negative term. The cultivation and development of knowledge of a nation with which Australia is so entwined, economically and otherwise, is surely necessary if we're to preserve our national interest in the course of negotiating that relationship.

Besides, nuanced does not mean uncritical. The CIW's flagship China Story Yearbook series, which I co-edit as a freelance editorial associate, includes essays on subjects such as cultural and political censorship in China, the ongoing clampdown on rights activism, and the mass incarceration and cultural suppression of Uyghers in Xinjiang. Which pandas, exactly, are being hugged here? The latest edition, *China Story Yearbook 2018: Power*, which like all the others is free to download from the CIW website, features a chapter by David Brophy titled "Australia's China Debate in 2018". In it, Brophy describes a marked shift towards polarisation in the discourse around China and discusses Hamilton's contribution to this change.

I never said that "quaking and shaking" *caused* what I characterise as "confounding and serious" issues in the bilateral relationship. But they don't help our ability to address them. Strategically, it is surely better to keep all lines of communication open, and to work at deepening our knowledge of this large and powerful country with whom Australia's fate is increasingly tied.

Of all the strange charges Hamilton levels at me, the notion that together with other members of my "in-group", I seek a "privileged role in explaining China to the rest of us" is the strangest. When did Hamilton, himself a university professor and author of numerous books and articles, decide that it's an undesirable thing for people who know something about a topic to speak up about it? As a freelance writer and editor, all my work on China has been about spreading and popularising knowledge, not owning or containing it; as a translator, I am proud of helping to introduce a range of Chinese voices, including those of poets, filmmakers, essayists and short-story writers, to Western audiences.

Hamilton accuses ill-intentioned "Sinologists" of trying to own the debate. Yet he's the one who seems to want to shut down – or shout down – the conversation. I too believe that our country should be vigilant and proactive in addressing all threats to its sovereignty and the integrity of its institutions. It's just that I don't think this precludes cultural engagement. You could say it mandates it. As Sunzi wrote in *The Art of War*, "Know yourself, and know your enemy, and you will not see defeat in a hundred battles."

Stay calm and study Chinese history.

Barry Li observes that many younger mainland-born Chinese today mistakenly believe that *The Red Detachment of Women* tells the story of the resistance to the Japanese occupation. This isn't especially surprising. There are so many gaps and distortions in the teaching of culture and history in the People's Republic, especially that of the Party itself, that I've met young people there who aren't sure if the Cultural Revolution occurred before or after "Liberation" in 1949.

In discussing his evolving views on Xinjiang, Li explains well the unconscious nature by which so much propaganda, including black-and-white views of the world, is absorbed. His understanding of the plight of the Uyghers changed when he came to Australia. This shift is in itself a testament to the power of cultural engagement. Li notes, as I have, that cultural engagement can be tricky and difficult, and it can raise the temperature of the conversation. But the point, really, is the conversation. As Li puts it so well, this is "how the 'art of democracy' differs fundamentally from the 'art of communism'".

Li makes a valid point about my lack of clear "recommendations and solutions". I would love to have been able to come up with more answers than questions. What's certain is that this country needs to find rational, effective and non-racialist ways of dealing with the challenges presented by an increasingly powerful and assertive China. This necessarily involves winning and keeping the confidence and loyalty of Australia's growing population of mainland-born Chinese. Australia must defend its sovereignty but without resorting to hysterical rhetoric that, in the end, could have the effect of alienating those we need, and many of whom themselves would prefer, to be held close.

Linda Jaivin, novelist, essayist, translator and
cultural commentator who writes frequently on China

Subscribe to Australian Foreign Affairs & save up to 28% on the cover price.

Enjoy free home delivery of the print edition and full digital access to the journal via the Australian Foreign Affairs website, iPad, iPhone and Android apps.

Forthcoming issue:
China Dependence: Australia's New Vulnerability (October 2019)

Never miss an issue. Subscribe and save.

☐ **1 year auto-renewing print and digital subscription** (3 issues) $49.99 within Australia. Outside Australia $79.99*

☐ **1 year print and digital subscription** (3 issues) $59.99 within Australia. Outside Australia $99.99

☐ **1 year auto-renewing digital subscription** (3 issues) $29.99.*

☐ **2 year print and digital subscription** (6 issues) $114.99 within Australia.

☐ Tick here to commence subscription with the current issue.

Give an inspired gift. Subscribe a friend.

☐ **1 year print and digital gift subscription** (3 issues) $59.99 within Australia. Outside Australia $99.99

☐ **1 year digital-only gift subscription** (3 issues) $29.99.

☐ **2 year print and digital gift subscription** (6 issues) $114.99 within Australia.

☐ Tick here to commence subscription with the current issue.

ALL PRICES INCLUDE GST, POSTAGE AND HANDLING.

*Your subscription will automatically renew until you notify us to stop. Prior to the end of your subscription period, we will send you a reminder notice.

Please turn over for subscription order form, or subscribe online at **australianforeignaffairs.com**
Alternatively, call 1800 077 514 or +61 3 9486 0288 or email **subscribe@australianforeignaffairs.com**

Back Issues

ALL PRICES INCLUDE GST, POSTAGE AND HANDLING.

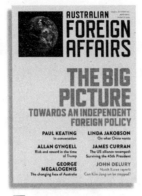

☐ **AFA1** ($15.99)
The Big Picture

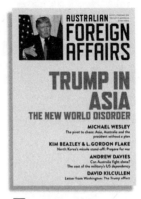

☐ **AFA2** ($15.99)
Trump in Asia

☐ **AFA3** ($15.99)
Australia & Indonesia

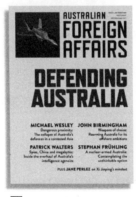

☐ **AFA4** ($22.99)
Defending Australia

☐ **AFA5** ($22.99)
Are We Asian Yet?

PAYMENT DETAILS I enclose a cheque/money order made out to Schwartz Publishing Pty Ltd. Or please debit my credit card (MasterCard, Visa or Amex accepted).

CARD NO.

EXPIRY DATE   /   CCV   AMOUNT $

CARDHOLDER'S NAME

SIGNATURE

NAME

ADDRESS

EMAIL   PHONE

Post or fax this form to: Reply Paid 90094, Carlton VIC 3053 **Freecall:** 1800 077 514 **or** +61 3 9486 0288
Fax: (03) 9011 6106 **Email:** subscribe@australianforeignaffairs.com **Website:** australianforeignaffairs.com
Subscribe online at australianforeignaffairs.com/subscribe (please do not send electronic scans of this form)

Until Sunday, 28 July, we are open for submissions on the topic of this issue, *Our Sphere of Influence*, to be published on the Australian Foreign Affairs website.

NEXT VOICES

The best new thinkers on Australian foreign affairs

Contributions must be 1500–2000 words and previously unpublished. Authors whose work is selected will receive AU$100 and a one-year print and digital subscription to Australian Foreign Affairs, and will collaborate with Australian Foreign Affairs editors to shape and refine their piece.

Writers do not have to be foreign-affairs experts: journalists, academics, foreign-aid workers, policy advisers, students and other interested readers are encouraged to submit. We seek to foster and promote a diverse stable of writers from Australia and the Asia-Pacific, and to encourage discussion on foreign affairs that represents a range of views in the broader Australian community.

To read our guidelines and submit,
visit australianforeignaffairs.com/next-voices

The Back Page

FINLANDISATION

What is it: A smaller power conciliating with a neighbouring hegemon. The term comes from Finland's relationship with Moscow after World War II. Without powerful allies, this small country, bordering the victorious USSR, needed to yield some sovereignty to avoid potential invasion.

Is it bad: Clifford G. Gaddy (senior fellow, Brookings Institution) calls it "a synonym for weak-kneed capitulationism", while Henry Kissinger (former Secretary of State, US) described it as a "balanced dissatisfaction" better than the alternatives. Perhaps the best description comes from Finland itself – Kari Suomalainen (cartoonist, Helsingin Sanomat) terms it "the art of bowing to the East so carefully that it could not be considered as mooning".

Where is it happening now: Supposedly everywhere. Ukraine is said to be at risk, again from Moscow. Robert D. Kaplan (managing director, Eurasia Group) says China will "Finlandize" South-East Asia, where governments will be nominally independent "but in the end abide by ... rules set by Beijing".

Peak Finlandisation: Max Boot (senior fellow, Council on Foreign Relations) claims US President Donald Trump "seems bent on the Finlandization of Europe – and even the United States".

Is there an alternative: Yes, but it may be worse. A close relative is "bandwagoning", coined by Quincy Wright (political scientist, University of Chicago) in 1942: where smaller states form military alignments with large, hostile neighbours to avoid defeat and benefit from future conquests.